Managing in the Email Office

To our respective parents Barbara and Cecil, Joyce and Harry

Managing in the Email Office

Monica E. Seeley
Gerard N. Hargreaves

OXFORD AMSTERDAM BOSTON LONDON NEW YORK PARIS
SAN DIEGO SAN FRANCISCO SINGAPORE SYDNEY TOKYO

Butterworth-Heinemann
An imprint of Elsevier Science
Linacre House, Jordan Hill, Oxford OX2 8DP
200 Wheeler Road, Burlington, MA 01803

First published 2003

British Library Cataloguing in Publication Data
A catalogue record for this book is available from the British Library

ISBN 0 7506 5698 0

For information on all Butterworth-Heinemann publications visit our website at www.bh.com

Composition by Genesis Typesetting, Rochester, Kent
Printed and bound in Great Britain

Contents

Computer Weekly Professional Series

There are few professions which require as much continuous updating as that of the IS executive. Not only does the hardware and software scene change relentlessly, but also ideas about the actual management of the IS function are being continuously modified, updated and changed. Thus keeping abreast of what is going on is really a major task.

The Butterworth-Heinemann – *Computer Weekly* Professional Series has been created to assist IS executives keep up to date with the management ideas and issues of which they need to be aware.

One of the key objectives of the series is to reduce the time it takes for leading edge management ideas to move from the academic and consulting environments into the hands of the IT practitioner. Thus this series employs appropriate technology to speed up the publishing process. Where appropriate some books are supported by CD-ROM or by additional information or templates located on the Web.

This series provides IT professionals with an opportunity to build up a bookcase of easily accessible, but detailed information on the important issues that they need to be aware of to successfully perform their jobs.

This book is also relevant to both the IT professional and the business user of IT systems.

Aspiring or already established authors are invited to get in touch with me directly if they would like to be published in this series.

Dan Remenyi

Dr Dan Remenyi
Series Editor
dan.remenyi@mcil.co.uk

Series Editor
Dan Remenyi, Visiting Professor, Trinity College Dublin

Other titles in the Series
Corporate politics for IT managers: how to get streetwise
Delivering IT and e-business value
eBusiness implementation
eBusiness strategies for virtual organizations
The effective measurement and management of IT costs and benefits
ERP: the implementation cycle
A hacker's guide to project management
How to become a successful IT consultant
How to manage the IT helpdesk
Information warfare: corporate attack and defence in a digital world
IT investment – making a business case
Knowledge management – a blueprint for delivery
Make or break issues in IT management
Making IT count
Network security
Prince 2: a practical handbook
The project manager's toolkit
Reinventing the IT department
Understanding the Internet

Foreword

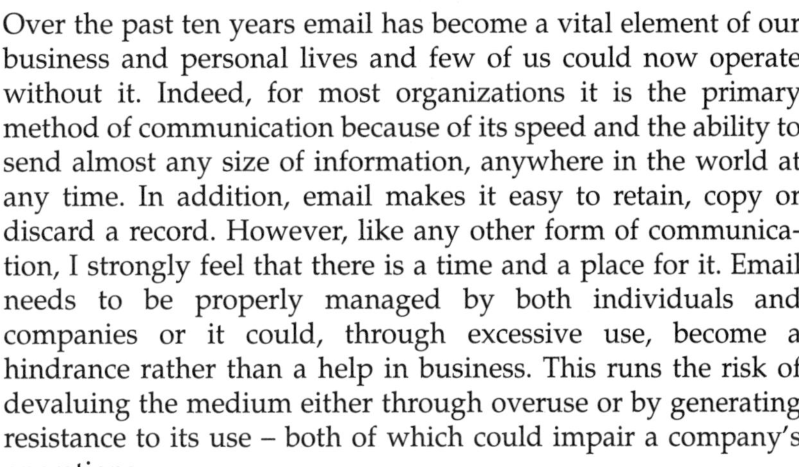

Over the past ten years email has become a vital element of our business and personal lives and few of us could now operate without it. Indeed, for most organizations it is the primary method of communication because of its speed and the ability to send almost any size of information, anywhere in the world at any time. In addition, email makes it easy to retain, copy or discard a record. However, like any other form of communication, I strongly feel that there is a time and a place for it. Email needs to be properly managed by both individuals and companies or it could, through excessive use, become a hindrance rather than a help in business. This runs the risk of devaluing the medium either through overuse or by generating resistance to its use – both of which could impair a company's operations.

We all need to take stock of when and how we use email – it's too easy to get addicted to your inbox and not really think about whether it is the most appropriate or productive method of communication in the circumstance. How often have you fired off an email response when picking up the phone might have worked better? How many times have you seen a businessman or woman waiting in a busy airport with their earpiece in, apparently madly talking to themselves while tapping away on their laptop sending emails and ignoring all around them. Is this really necessary? Far better to talk to a competitor than risk a leak of sensitive information to that same competitor by using a laptop in an open area.

Like any other aspect of management the effective use of IT requires continuous learning and the updating of skills. Taking time to read this book will be repaid many times over.

Sir Colin Chandler, Chairman, easyJet

Preface

Why read this book?

This book will show you not only how to survive in the email office but how to come out winning. Email is now one of the top ten causes of work-related stress. Little wonder, when you realize that on average we all receive one new email every 15 minutes of the normal working day. For some this can even be as high as one every three minutes.

The first ever email was sent in 1971. It is only in the last ten years though that emails have become such an integral part of our lives. The equivalent of 360 000 emails are sent every second in Britain today, representing a 20 per cent growth of internet traffic in recent months alone. The peak daily level is reached late afternoon and early evening. This reflects partly the changing work environment from a traditional nine to five, five days a week to 24×7×365 and the growth in usage of computer technology at home. There are now over 8 million households in Britain with web access and over 120 internet service providers in Britain. Email is growing at a rapid rate and the number of person-to-person emails sent on an average day is predicted to exceed 36 billion worldwide in 2005.

Yet despite the havoc it causes to many people's carefully planned working day and total work–life balance, email is a powerful enabler. It transforms not only the work we do but also the way we do it. Many people feel their inbox has spiralled out of control and that it now manages them rather than the other way around. However, just a look at the content of an inbox and how the owner manages (or does not manage) that inbox reveals a great deal about both the person and the organization they work for. *Your inbox is a fingerprint of you as a manager and of your organization's culture.* Know yourself and your organization and you can learn to take control of your inbox. This will lead you to use email more successfully, which in turn will increase both your personal productivity and that of your organization.

Regardless of whether you handle your own email or delegate tasks, email now touches the lives of nearly everyone who works, from a receptionist in a small company to the chairman of a large multinational corporation. The extent to which it has invaded our lives depends on many factors. Among those of you in senior positions, some will handle their own inbox, while others will delegate that task to a personal assistant (or secretary). Nonetheless, as a member of the top management team, even if you are not a frequent direct user yourself, you may have responsibility for ensuring email is used properly as part of the overall corporate communications strategy and is in keeping with the image of the company.

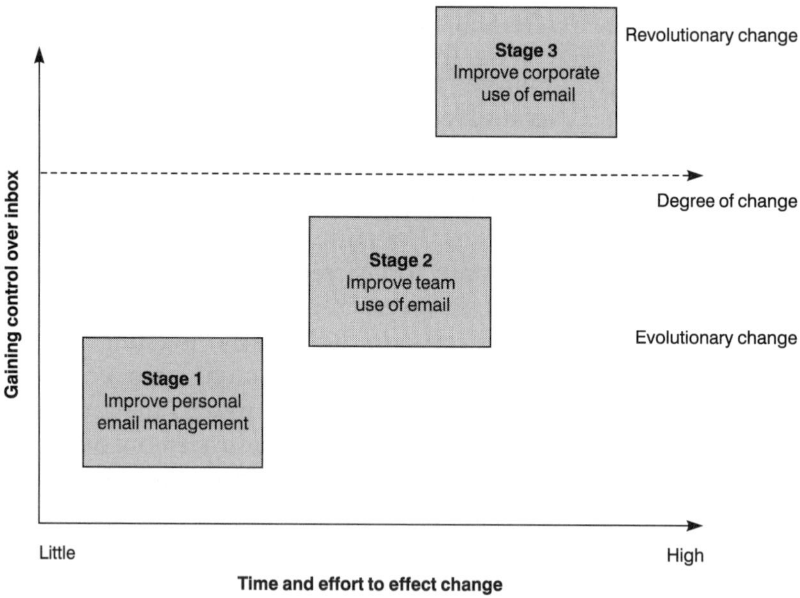

Figure i
Managing your inbox before it manages you

Winning the battle with email and containing the shower of new emails is a three-stage process as shown in Figure i.

First, you need to improve your personal effectiveness as an email user and become a good email citizen. Second, having established the role model for how a well-respected email citizen behaves, you need to influence those you work most closely with, to adopt similar principles of best practice. Third, you need to work towards changing the overall corporate attitude towards email and the way it is used.

Improving your own personal email management techniques will result in at least a 25 per cent efficiency gain. This will be in terms of time saved using email and by being right first time. That is to say, putting across your message, finding information and receiving just the email you need – no more no less. Fostering and engendering a similar change among your immediate team can provide a further 10 to 15 per cent efficiency . You should see a further reduction in the volume of email traffic in and out of your inbox.

The first two stages are evolutionary as you are essentially in control certainly of your own destiny and to some degree that of your team (or department). Stages 1 and 2 generally require some small change to existing management processes and they may require you to rethink how you work and communicate with your immediate team members; whereas at the corporate level you may be looking at a fundamental change in perceptions and behaviours. Email is often just the wallpaper covering up much deeper organizational problems and mismatches between the espoused values and those in practice and especially openness.

Creating email best practice across the organization, as a whole, is therefore often the hardest part but it will add at least another 25 per cent gain in efficiency and resource allocation. This is achieved mainly through the savings in people's time spent dealing with email and the hardware resources needed to process and store all the emails.

Who is the book for?

This book is for those who are constantly trying to protect themselves from the torrential downpour of new and often unwanted email and those who have responsibility for how email is used across a team, division or the organization as a whole.

The principles of email best practice are independent of organizational size, sector, systems in use and position. Therefore this book is for users from:

- all levels in the organization, from chief executive to receptionist;
- all functions of the organization such as marketing, information technology, personnel, sales, logistics, customer service, engineering and research;
- all levels of technical expertise (from beginners to very experienced users) and working with all types of email software and systems;
- all sectors, for example, pubic sector, private sector, professional organizations such as accountants and lawyers, academic institutes and charities;
- all sizes of organizations from a micro-organization of one to two people to small to medium size enterprises (SMEs) and large FTSE 100 organizations.

Why? Because many of the ways to leverage email as a management tool are basically grounded in sound management practices. They are independent of the technology you have in place. Using email effectively depends on you knowing what you want to achieve as an individual and what you want to achieve for your organization.

What will you gain from reading this book?

This book is about how to leverage the power of email as a business management tool. What you learn will prevent you from being so buried by your email that you lose sight of your business strategy. The contents of this book are designed to help you:

- save time dealing with your inbox;
- reduce the information overload stress factor;
- decrease the number of emails you handle;
- communicate more expediently by email;
- develop quicker ways to share and manage information using email;
- be more productive using email;
- identify ways to use email to support your preferred working style;
- stop email disrupting your work–life balance;
- set the role model for being a good email citizen;

- create best practice within your immediate team;
- enhance the way you and your secretary handle your inbox;
- establish best practice across the organization.

Structure of this book

Taking control of the inbox and exploiting the potential power of email is a three-stage process as outlined. This book is in three parts, which reflect this model.

Part One – Managing your email before it manages you

This will provide you with ways to improve your own personal techniques for managing your inbox. It covers how to manage yourself as an email user and how to use the technology to do so.

Part Two – You and your team in the email office

This is about how to work email and your inbox as a management tool for working more effectively as a team, whether as a two-person team of manager and PA or a larger team.

Part Three – The corporate perspective

This part focuses on what to do to establish best practice across a complete organization, be that a division, subsidiary, or the corporation as a whole. This includes an email citizens charter which is a set of nine suggested guidelines for what we believe comprises the hallmark of personal email best practice from a behavioural and management perspective. It closes with a look at how we might be working with email in the future.

How can I gain the maximum value from reading this book

In addition to the core content, most chapters contain case histories and some self-assessment exercises and instruments. To gain the maximum value from reading each chapter you should work your way though these exercises. They are designed to help you identify strengths and weaknesses as an email user and hence where and how you could develop your skills to improve yourself (or your team and organization as appropriate).

Each chapter finishes with a summary and often a quick reference guide in the form of quick tips and hints. These can be used as personal reminders to help you as you master and implement the relevant parts of the book on your journey to becoming a better email user.

Acknowledgements

This book could not have been written without the help of the many executives who opened up their inboxes (and often their hearts) to us to talk about how they managed their email. Thank you for sharing with us your highs and lows and the delights and the frustrations of using email.

We are most grateful to the many expert users who provided us with ideas and insights into the world of managing by email and especially Lynn Clarke of Lafarge Aggregates, Will Brown of Telecom One, Steve Dobson of Giga (for providing us with key briefing papers), Rebecca George and Dave Snowden of IBM, Simon Peach of Executive Lifestyle Computing, Kerstin Reiners of Clearswift, Brian Sutton of Ufi/learndirect, and Carmel Swann of the Department for Education and Skills.

Some of the initial impetus for this work came from Sir Michael Bichard who asked the question 'how can I reduce the volume of email . . .'. Thank you for the challenge.

Part of the research for this book was undertaken by students at the Business School, Imperial College London: we appreciate Professor David Targett's insightful guidance and those who carried out the research on our behalves.

All authors need a helping hand and someone who believes in them. We thank John Riley and Ross Bentley of *Computer Weekly* for their inspiration and persuading us to take the plunge.

Writing this book was a team effort. We are eternally grateful to Lorna Campbell for acting as a model team manager being gentle but firm and editing each chapter to ensure that there was continuity, to Grant Springford for all the illustrations which he did in his spare time for the love of email and art, and to Susan

Oakes of the London Mathematical Society for providing us with a meeting room and an endless supply of coffee, and to our excellent editors Mike Cash and Jennifer Wilkinson of Butterworth-Heinemann for their patience and support.

Unlike the old days when a letter was carefully written, considered, read and re-read before sealing and mailing, now we are clicking and sending notes as fast as our fingers can race across the keyboard . . . Like Queen Victoria we can use the written word to express ourselves articulately and with more authority.

Michael Eisner, Chairman, Walt Disney
Financial Times, 2 May 2000

Part One

Managing your email before it manages you

I find that I automatically filter my emails. I don't even think about it. I get down a screen of red email and I go down and I can see immediately the third I don't need to deal with . . . People have different ways of coping with it [the red tidal wave of new email] but I've found that you do have to have a mechanism for filtering your mail or else you go bonkers.

Director, Business Division,
international computer services organization

This quote typifies how many users feel about email. Some people feel they cannot even take a holiday without checking their email at some point. Whether this is right or wrong is another matter. Taking control of your inbox and learning to manage it rather than letting it manage your life at work and away from work involves a combination of sound personal management practices and appropriate level of email IT fitness (that is, competence and confidence with the technology). It is about knowing what information you really need, feeling secure and not worrying about having all the 'nice to know' stuff, and properly managing the time you spend dealing with your email.

Part One is about you as an individual user. It will look at what you alone can do to surf the tidal wave of new email and in particular it will help you to:

- measure the level of email overload to which you are subjected;
- benchmark your level of email IT fitness and email management style;

- appreciate how your use of email and the volume of email you receive relates directly to your preferred pattern of work and style of management;
- recognize what might be your strengths and weaknesses as an email user;
- develop your strengths and overcome your weaknesses as an email user;
- audit your inbox to identify how you could reduce the volume of emails you receive;
- learn how to reduce and manage the stress associated with email and information overload;
- be aware of what aspects of the use of email you can control and where you need to influence other people's email behaviour.

Successfully and efficiently making email work for you as a business communications and knowledge management tool truly embodies the principle of 'doing unto others as you would be done by'. You cannot expect others to behave as good email users if you behave badly and either shower them with unwanted emails or ignore those you receive.

This part of the book contains a selection of self-assessment exercises to help you benchmark how well you personally manage your inbox. There are tips and hints on how to improve in order to save yourself and others, time and energy dealing with email, and to use email more productively.

1 Taking control of your inbox

How can I reduce the volume of email I handle each day?
Do I need to change the way others use emails with me?
How can I take control of my inbox rather than it controlling me?

1.1 Introduction

The two questions, most frequently asked of us, are:

> 'How can I reduce the tidal wave of email I receive each day?'
> 'Why do I feel as if my inbox is managing me – what can I do?'

The solution to both questions requires some simple but firm changes. To paraphrase that famous song, you will need 'a little help from your friends' and from your colleagues. When you decide to change your behaviour, regardless of why, and what that behaviour constitutes it will have some form of ripple effect on those around you. For example, if you decide to stop smoking, you may be grumpy en route to achieving your goal. Perhaps you have chosen to manage your time better. This may mean changing the time you have available for different people.

The same applies to reducing the volume of email you handle each day. A large part of the solution lies in your own hands in terms of you becoming a better email citizen. However, the full extent of your success will also depend in part on how others you work with use email. When an organization decides to effect a change in how it and its employees behave there is usually a corporate change management programme and initiative. Similarly, when a company decides to improve its quality control processes, there will be an organization-wide training and development strategy and protocols designed to handle any resulting new process.

Keeping email under control requires a careful balance of common sense, organizational skills and vigilant workplace policy. One aspect of this is evidenced by employers who now implement strict rules for deleting email. This not only helps employees but also saves the company spiralling data storage costs and offers legal protection. So to make real headway with your inbox you need to make sure your company and colleagues are involved.

Email has become the DNA of communications and to some extent knowledge management. Yet, very few organizations ensure this valuable resource is used wisely. Few even realize that part of the problem lies not with the individual but with the corporate culture and how information and management are perceived. Many organizations talk about having an apolitical culture where trust is the byword and that its workforce is empowered. Yet, a cursory look at a sample of their middle manager's inboxes will reveal a high percentage of copied (cc'd) emails. This is because the manager is still seen as the hub and the ultimate controller of power. Everyone is playing 'cover my backside'.

Reducing the tidal wave of incoming emails depends not only on how you manage your inbox but also on getting your colleagues to act responsibly. This includes both your immediate team (and/or department) and the organization as a whole.

This chapter explodes some common myths associated with the size of your inbox and the time you need to spend dealing with it. It provides a more reliable way to measure email overload. It gives you an overview and the Mesmo three-stage model (three steps to effective personal email management – Figure 1.5, page

14), which shows you how you can reduce the time spent dealing with your inbox without suffering any loss of information or ability to communicate effectively. Indeed, it highlights the opposite. Take control of your inbox and encourage others to do the same and you can quickly become better informed, a more effective communicator and save yourself time.

1.2 Exploding the myths of size and time

1.2.1 So you think you have a bulging inbox?

What constitutes a high volume of email traffic? For one manager this might mean 25 incoming emails per day and for another it could be 125. You might be the European operations director of a large technology company and receive about 100 emails a day because of the nature of your job, the global span of your responsibilities and your organization's heavy dependence on email. It is not unusual for a senior director in a government agency to receive an average of 120 emails at certain points in the week, notably Fridays, when ministers clear the decks for the weekend. On the other hand one managing director of an international software house feels he is overwhelmed if he receives more than about 15 emails a day, as he actively encourages people to talk and use the intranet to share information rather than email.

Figure 1.1 shows the average number of emails received by a group of ten managers (whom we studied) each from different organizations which range from a medium sized PR company to

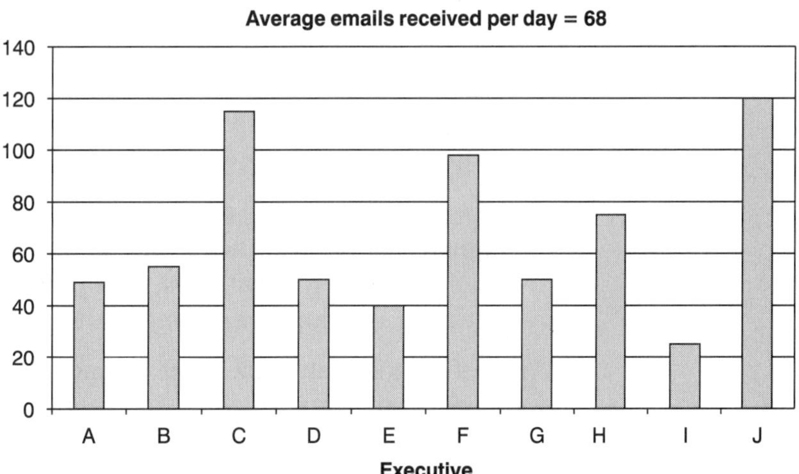

Figure 1.1
A day in the life of an executive's inbox

Table 1.1 A typical day in the life of an executive's inbox

Executive	Volume	Title	Organization
A	49	Director European operation	International software solutions company
B	55	Managing director	Public relations company
C	115	Managing director	Public relations company
D	50	Vice president marketing	International software development organization
E	40	Manager public relations – EMEA	International telecommunications organization
F	98	European operations director	International technology hardware manufacturer
G	50	IT director	Automobile parts manufacturer
H	75	Chief technology officer	Telecommunications organization
I	25	General manager	International software and services supplier
J	120	Director	Government agency
Average	**67.7**		

the director of a division of a major government agency as summarized in Table 1.1.

While the average number of received emails was 68, this masked terrific swings from the general manager (I) who only received 25 to the senior director of the division of government agency (J) who received 120. The number of sent items is generally about a third of what is received.

This certainly begs the question about who else is sending all that email? What is always fascinating is the gap between perceptions and reality. Most people have a tendency to overestimate the number of emails they receive.

Without looking at your inbox, guess what you think is the average throughput for your inbox. Now take a more object measurement and actually count the number received and sent.

> **Your inbox traffic**
> Number received
> Number sent yesterday
> How does it compare to those in our study?
> How do you feel this compares to others in your organization/ division?

To some extent therefore comparisons are meaningless, although there is evidence to suggest that men are more likely than women to boast about the size of their inbox. Some senior executives almost boast about the size of their inbox and the quantity of daily emails they receive, thinking of it as a sign that they must be really busy and important. Of course those who are good email citizens will know that what really counts is the ratio of noise to information. Before we look at this all-important ratio and explore just exactly what is influencing the traffic let's explode one other major myth about handling your inbox – the time it takes.

1.2.2 Are you spending too long on email?

Comparison of time spent handling email is another of those mythical nonsensical yardsticks that is bandied around and used to make people feel really depressed. Please, don't misread us. We all, probably, spend far too long clicking the keys of our PC firing off emails and in effect engaging our fingers before our brain. The trouble with comparisons and measures of time is that although it's very comforting to know that you are within striking distance of your peers, they really are only comfort blankets. In reality the time someone else spends on her inbox tells you nothing about whether that same time is correct for you, and your role and organization. The DTI recently found that people spend on average 49 minutes per day working with emails. Spending one to two hours might be nearer the mark for some and indeed quite proper for their job:

> *I get 60 or so emails in a day. Most are people asking can I do this and me saying yes or no. Four or five will require going away and proper thinking to draw up a proper reply.*
>
> Lisa, head of personnel, government agency

> *I receive about 50 emails a day. One group would be about being informed – updates on projects I am interested in. Others are operational information. Then there is personnel – i.e. employment sort of things. But what takes the most time is the day-to-day projects (I am involved in six), i.e. briefings, being asked to make*

decisions, asking others to make decisions. All this is interspersed with conference calls or one-to-one telephone calls then an email that confirms what went on.

Stephen, business development manager, international software supplier

The time you spend dealing with your inbox will depend on the volume of emails, but more fundamentally the nature and complexity of the emails. Some managers can easily find themselves spending up to three hours per night dealing with it in addition to time spent in the office handling the really urgent ones. Whereas others get by in short sharp bursts of no more than an hour at the end of the day.

1.2.3 Busting the time myth

Don't stress yourself out by trying to calibrate yourself against others. What you need to think about is how can you personally save time or invoke the help of others to help you save time. Being aware of who and what is causing the congestion in your inbox will help you reduce the volume and time you spend dealing with your inbox.

1.3 What do we really mean by information overload?

Nobody heard him, the dead man,
But still he lay moaning:
I was much further out than you thought
And not waving but drowning.

Stevie Smith (1975) 'Not Waving but Drowning'

You wake up on Monday knowing you still have a hangover of at least 60 unread emails from last week. By the time you arrive at your office the red tidal wave of unopened emails will probably be washing over you. The week hasn't even begun and already you feel like that character from the famous Stevie Smith poem, 'Not Waving but Drowning'.

How do you know if you have email overload? The number of emails and the time spent dealing with them is not in itself an effective measure. A more realistic measure is what we call information to noise ratio.

1.3.1 Information to noise ratio

What is undisputable is that most people's inboxes contain far too much noise. **Noise is those emails you receive which are of no interest or importance to you.** That is, irrelevant, trivial extraneous messages about which you have little or no interest. Yes, data not information. An audit of one quite typical senior executive revealed that of 160 emails over 45 per cent were information with no sell-by date (see Figure 1.2). This means the email was sent to him with no specific time by which he needed to read it – therefore most was unread and would be deleted.

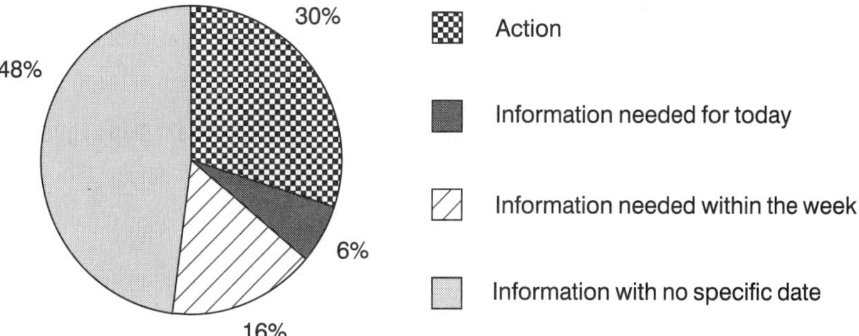

Figure 1.2
Noise and information

Noisy emails are the ones which you either flick open or even go straight past. You may wonder why you have been sent it in the first place and proceed to bin without hesitation. They are the emails which linger at the bottom of your inbox, unsorted and maybe even unread. They include junk mail, e-newsletters which have lost their appeal and ones from colleagues who just sent you the email because they felt you really ought to know what they were doing and talking about.

Information, by contrast, is represented by the emails you feel add value to your executive lifestyle and *modus operandi*. They enable you to perform your role more effectively. For example, by improving your decision making you are better informed about your market place and your team's work, helping you manage a project, enhancing your relationship with your clients, and so on. They are the emails that form an essential part of your daily diet of killer information which helps you perform your job (whether you are part of a formal corporate team or self-employed but working with others).

What we call email overload is the point when your inbox starts to contain a high percentage of noise to information. A more precise scale of email overload is shown in Figure 1.3.

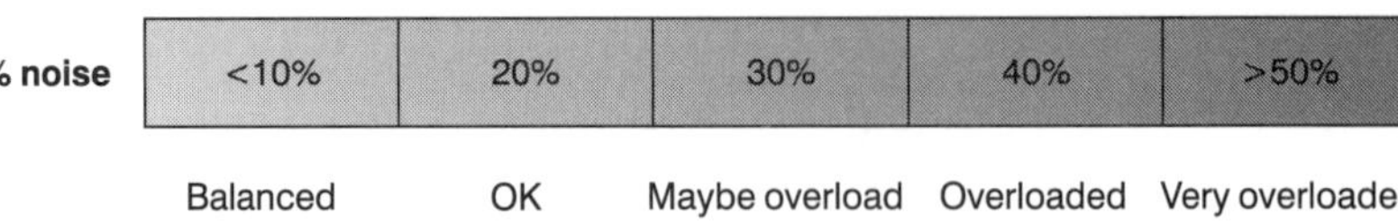

Figure 1.3
The inbox information overload scale

This is the true measure of email overload, which leads to information overload and stress. When your inbox contains more than 30 per cent noise (regardless of the overall volume of email) that is when you will start to feel email overload. Sadly, many managers' inboxes contain a diet of low information and high noise, when what you need to run your business is low noise and high information. What you should be thinking about therefore is how to redress the balance (assuming there is an inbalance).

We all need some distractions in life. It is impossible for most of us to stay focused on one piece of work all day, especially if it is a hard thought-provoking task. For many the noise in their inbox just represents a light-hearted break. However, the problem with the noisy inbox is that it is in all probability consuming precious energy and time, which could be better used.

> **My inbox and the ratio of noise to information**
> Think about your current inbox, what percentage do you think is noise?
> Who and how is all this noise being generated and how can you redress the balance?

Remember those old fashioned chats we all used to have around the coffee machine? Or stopping to read a newspaper or even phoning someone? With a high level of noise the temptation is to turn away from these richer and possibly more rewarding sources of rejuvenation to stay glued to the shallow, faceless world of our inbox.

1.4 Who's making demands on my inbox and creating a noise?

The volume of traffic in your inbox will depend on a number of interrelated factors, as shown in Figure 1.4. The volume of traffic through your inbox will be a reflection of:

- you and your personal work habits (dictated to some degree by factors such as your role, information needs and management style);

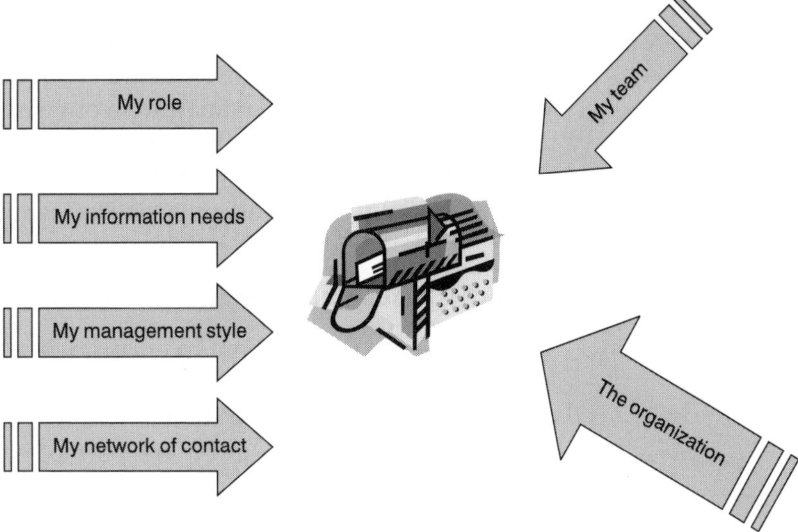

Figure 1.4
Who's making demands on my inbox?

- how your team perceives email should be used;
- the organizational culture with respect to email.

We will explore these briefly and revisit them in more detail in Chapter 12.

1.4.1 You and your executive lifestyle

No two managers will ever perform the same job in an identical manner. We all have different management styles, roles, relationships that we value, communications patterns and information needs. These are the attributes that comprise your executive lifestyle, and these will influence how you use IT in general, and more specifically email, as indicated in the introduction. (See Seeley (2000) for a review of the relationship between executive lifestyle and use of the PC.)

The first person making demands on your inbox is you. Are you the sort of manager who like to micro-manage and be involved to a lesser or greater degree in every project? Or do you prefer to stand back and delegate and make space for others to shine through? How extensive is your network of contacts? How well do you work that network? Are you very selective about what you read, or are you an information junkie drinking in any news that is available? The answer to all these questions (and others about how you manage) will affect the size of your inbox and the time it takes you to manage it.

Ways to save time depending on your executive lifestyle are discussed in Chapters 2 and 3. However, as you will see there are several common sense tactics you can employ to help yourself. For example, managing your time better, tempering the temptation to rush to the inbox instead of talking and last but not least, making the time to audit your inbox to identify what you really need and what is irrelevant.

1.4.2 Your team's perception of email

The word team is used here to encompass all those for who you have overall management responsibility, from a small group to an entire department for which you are the manager. If you work either on your own or are part of a team, it is taken to imply those with whom you work directly.

To a large extent, not surprisingly, your management and communications style will dictate how people communicate with you through email. For example, do you want to be copied in on all dialogues relating to all projects? Whether you are managing an entire business division or a small team, have you stated what you see as acceptable protocols for using email? Managers often talk about the amount of emails they receive that they do not want and then have to spend time deleting them. They complain that a large proportion of their inbox is the result of the excessive use of 'reply all' and the 'cc' box. However, very few actually provide clear guidelines of the email behaviour they want members of their team to exhibit.

Cries of despair and deleting mountains of unwanted email are rather like cutting off the leaves on a rose that has been blighted by greenfly. What you have to do is systemically deter any unwanted aphides to have a healthy plant, i.e. you need to destroy their eggs before they can even hatch. You must do the same with email. We are not talking about typical junk mail but rather all those emails members of your team send you because they think you want or need to see them. They do it because there has been no word or order to the contrary and they are 'protecting their backs'.

1.4.3 The organizational culture

It is surprising how few organizations proactively promote email best practice and have clear well-established standards and guidelines. So it's hardly a surprise that email floods the communications systems and people are drowning in noise rather than information. Moreover, as we will see, aspects of the organizational culture can also affect the flow of emails such as:

- information culture (pushing information out rather than an individual pulling information to him or her as needed);
- prevailing structure (e.g. task, power, bureaucracy or people based);
- levels of uncertainty within the organization (due to change, i.e. mergers, redundancies);
- other available information sharing systems (e.g. intranets and personal portals).

For example, in a bureaucracy, inboxes are likely to have a high level of cc'd mail which for some may constitute simply noise. And similarly a push information culture will drive up the throughput. Uncertainty during a takeover bid or restructuring can cause the inbox to start to bulge, as Ruth explains:

> *There is a feeling that everyone needs to tell everyone what they are doing because they don't understand what everyone else is doing and who is responsible for what. By telling everyone you hope you have probably told the right person.*
>
> Ruth Daniel, head of human resources, international business services organization

Chapter 12 contains a more detailed discussion on how to spot these deviations and deal with them. At this stage the key point is to note that the enormity of traffic though your personal inbox will be determined by a combination of these three factors, namely your:

- executive lifestyle;
- team's preconceptions about you and email;
- organization's prevailing corporate culture.

The question now is how can you reduce any email overload and save time dealing with your inbox?

1.5 Ways to reduce information overload

Gaining control of your inbox and learning to surf the tidal wave of new emails is a three-stage process as outlined in the preface in Figure i. This is the initial stage over which you have

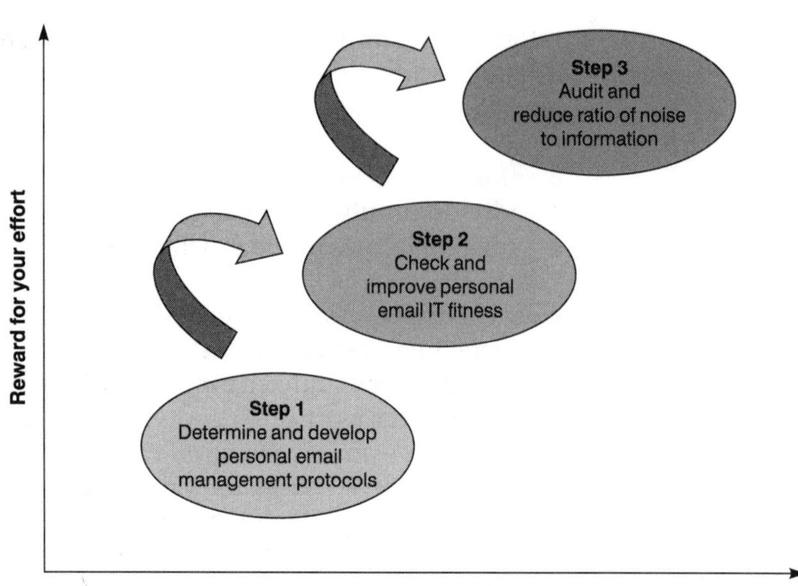

Figure 1.5
The Mesmo model for effective personal email management

total and absolute control. As illustrated in Figure 1.5, this is a simple three-step process to effective email management:

Step 1 – Check you are managing your email time effectively.
Step 2 – Ensure you are using the full potential of the technology.
Step 3 – Audit the noise to information level of your inbox.

Step 1 is to ensure you are managing yourself effectively in terms of the time you spend handling your inbox. Have you prioritized where email fits in your day and what priority you place on which emails? Are you a good email citizen who is able to manage their inbox efficiently and use email to work productively with others? Step 2 is to make sure you leverage the full power of the email software to match your email management style. All email software has a number of built-in time-saving features and functions. The question is are you working at the right level of email IT fitness to operate the software to maximum capacity? Step 3 is about being ruthless and auditing your inbox to decide just what it is you really need to receive. This is the hard part as we all have this innate fear that we might just miss something of importance.

If you improve your personal techniques for managing email (steps 1 and 2) you can expect to see a 10 to 20 per cent gain in efficiency and correspondingly reduce any email overload. If you then audit your inbox to evaluate the ratio of noise to information you will see a further improvement of about 15 to 25 per cent.

1.6 Summary

The only real measure of whether you are suffering true email overload is to measure the percentage of noise in your inbox. If you want to reduce the volume of traffic through your inbox, you must first improve your level of email IT fitness and your personal management processes. Then (or at the same time) audit your inbox to determine the ratio of noise to information. Having done this the next way to gain an improvement and further reduce any information overload is to reassess how you use email within your team. The last step is changing or at least establishing adequate organizational processes and procedures and these are discussed in Part Three.

2 What your inbox says about you

Is there a correlation between the content of my inbox and my information needs?
How does the content of my inbox reflect my management style?
What does the content of my inbox say about my communications preferences?

2.1 Introduction

To a large extent your inbox is a fingerprint of both you and your organization's culture. On the micro scale it reflects your:

- management style;
- information needs;
- communications preferences;
- patterns of work;
- work–life balance.

At the macro level your inbox echoes the ethos of the organization and especially its:

- style of management;
- value and culture of information management;
- communications processes and preferences;
- ethical values;
- approach to flexible working and work–life balance;
- use of technology.

In this chapter we will build upon the foundations laid out in Chapter 1 and explore how you can attune your preferred executive lifestyle (*modus operandi*) to:

- build on your personal strengths to help manage your inbox more efficiently and save time;
- acknowledge how your weaknesses might work against you when managing your inbox and cost you time and create stress.

The relationship with the corporate culture is dealt with in Chapter 12. In this chapter the focus is on you and your management lifestyle. We will look at how you can develop some personal management protocols to help you manage more effectively in the world of email (Step 1 of the Mesmo model of better email management).

2.2 The picture of me painted by my inbox

Most people's inbox fall into one of the four quadrants of the noise to information matrix shown in Figure 2.1. As indicated this, along with the way you handle the incumbent email, gives a snapshot of your overall working habits. For example, those with a high level of noise and information are often email addicts. They often take a scattergun approach to communications and may be poor in general at managing their time and at identifying just what information they really need for their job.

In contrast those who have a low noise–low information inbox often have a more planned and relaxed management style. They place a high value on face-to-face communications and are often not very good with IT to the point of being almost technophobic.

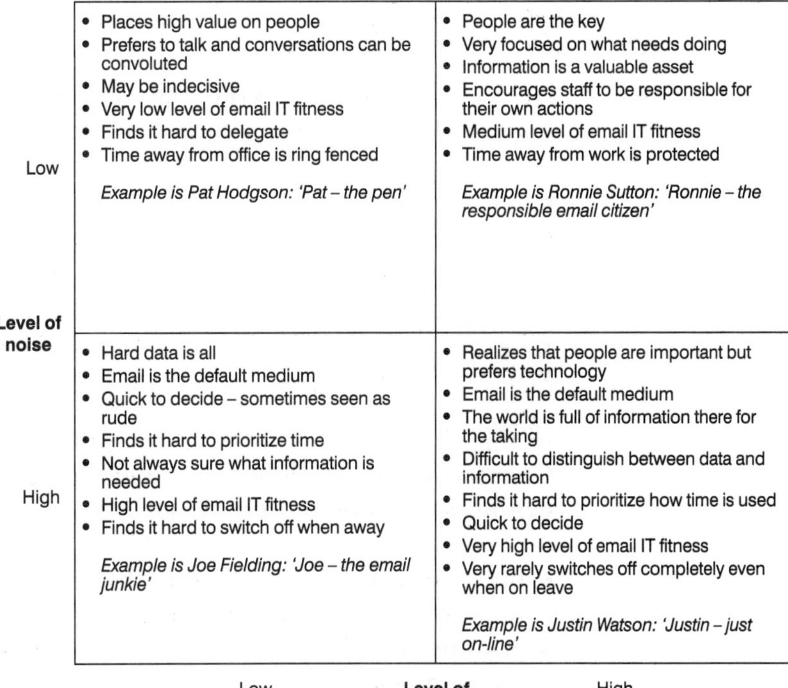

Figure 2.1
Typical management styles and the noise to information matrix

We will look at a typical day in the life a person whose inbox represents each one of the quadrants to see:

- what it tells us about that type of inbox;
- how you could save some time and work smarter with email.

2.3 Case history – Pat Hodgson (low noise/low information)

2.3.1 Pat – the pen

Pat begins the day in a very leisurely fashion helping to get the children up and taking time to sit down for breakfast with the family. Pat likes to take his time and enjoy life.

Pat likes to allow plenty of time to get to the office. The car has a good radio/CD player and the relaxed drive to work is time well spent keeping abreast of world events by listening to the news. He's never worked out how to use the CD changer so that remains unused, unless his kids load his favourite music up for him.

On arrival in the office Pat spends some time chatting to the secretary and other members of the team under the guise of a daily briefing. Pat has never been a fan of the computer and regrets the day email arrived in the office.

While Pat is happy giving general direction, decisions are rarely made without a lot of deliberation. How can you do this effectively without talking things through face to face or at least a telephone call? He really enjoys meetings but if Pat is in charge they can go on. He is known to be somewhat long-winded and one of his colleagues describes his style as 'Why use two words when you can use twenty'.

Once Pat gets into the office, focus is the key thing. Powers of concentration are impressive and Pat's eye for detail sometimes borders on the fanatical. His favourite lament is: 'Do I have to do everything myself?' He is fearful of delegating too much and really would prefer, if time permitted, to do everything himself. His computer, which IT insisted on connecting to the office network, sits on a spare desk in the corner of the office. The main desk is full of important paperwork, an in-tray, pending tray and an outbox plus a pile of unread magazines and journals. Pat refuses to allow technology to be the driving force and gets very frustrated at people who cannot be bothered to walk across the office or along the corridor to talk to colleagues personally rather than always sending emails. It has become a standing joke in the office that Pat rarely opens emails, personally leaving it to the secretary to print off important messages and leave them on the desk.

Pat has tried but he finds it so impersonal that he would only open emails once or twice a week. He just can't believe that people need to spend hours every day sending and receiving emails when in many cases a quick phone call or meeting with all parties concerned would solve the issue. Pat gets frustrated that most of the messages seem to be from people copying his name on every thing. 'It wouldn't happen if they kept to paper copies.'

Pat is a popular boss and colleague but his refusal to embrace the world of technology frustrates them. In addition to a reluctance to use email Pat rarely uses PowerPoint for his presentations or the electronic diary system. Booking a meeting with Pat can be a long process, having to go through his secretary first. He has had plenty of opportunity to learn but it has become something of a point of principal. 'We are a people business and that's the best way to communicate.'

Business trips and time away from the office have always been precious for Pat. This is thinking time. Pat will use the mobile phone and is meticulous at returning calls. The line is drawn on holidays though. Holidays are a time for the family and the phone stays switched off. There are too many reports of stressed executives taking their laptops and mobile phones on holiday for Pat to even contemplate this.

Pat does secretly worry that he is getting left behind as business becomes reliant on technology. One day he must change . . . but where to start?

2.3.2 What is revealed about Pat's executive lifestyle?

Management style

A relaxed and open style of management
Sometimes procrastinates
Engenders calm and trust among his team and subordinates
Popular to a point

Information needs

Not always clear about what information he really needs
Finds it hard to throw away old papers and magazines

IT fitness

Bronze level – slightly technophobic
Likes paper
Depends on his secretary to handle his inbox

Communications patterns

Prefers face-to-face communications, e.g. meetings
Meetings can be unstructured
Discussions may be verbose and rambling

Work–life balance

Home life is important
A firm believer in disconnecting from the world of work when on leave

2.3.3 How could Pat make email add more value to his work life?

First and foremost Pat should try to recast his thinking about email and the use of an electronic calendar. He should increase his personal level of email IT fitness. This would help him feel more comfortable with the technology in general. He is right to believe that it is the people that count, but his disdain for email may be causing his team as much stress as the person who overuses it. Pat should start to cultivate using email for the short non-equivocal communications, e.g. booking a meeting, saying yes or no to a request.

His ability to concentrate means he should find it easy to allocate specific times in the day when he will deal with his email, and his staff will need to recognize that just because he is on-line doesn't mean they will be replied to any more quickly. Pat's eye for detail could be a double-edged sword. It will mean that his emails will be properly worded (no typos, email shorthand or staccato messages from Pat). However, this means that it will take him far longer to send an email than is necessary. A compromise might be needed.

To date, no top manager has missed out on promotion because they don't use email, but increasingly it is becoming an unwritten rule that you can use email and especially as more and more companies operate in the 7×24×365 space. The longer Pat leaves it to join the world of email the harder he will find it to embrace as part of his *modus operandi* – he might just be jeopardizing his future career prospects.

2.4 Case history – Joe Fielding (high noise/low information)

2.4.1 Joe – the email junkie

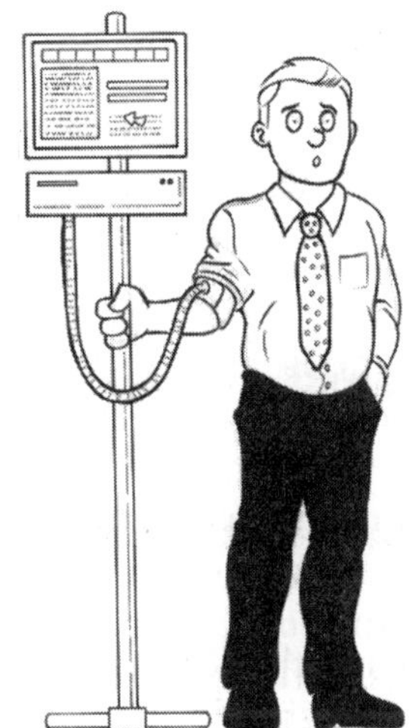

Joe is up and out of the house in 15 or 20 minutes depending on whether ironed clothes can be found. Breakfast is snatched from the toaster on the way out the door. Joe hates hanging around when there is work to be done.

Joe has a 45-minute train commute which gives time to fire off responses to overnight emails from the New York office. Joe is known by colleagues as 'an email junkie'.

Being the first in the office, he has a coffee and finishes the overnight emails. Joe hates long 'waffley' emails – more than four lines and he loses concentration. Brevity and speed are key to Joe's communications, both verbal and electronic. Most responses are a swift yes or no. Anything more complicated waits in the inbox until later. He is a busy man, time is key. He is always in a rush and everything is done at a run. However, he has to get his email 'fix' and dips in and out of his email all day long.

Joe likes to be in the know and insists on being copied in on all the departmental activities. 'The bigger the inbox, the busier the office', is one of Joe's many mottos. However, you will not be surprised to learn that his sent box is even bigger. Joe really believes that the number of emails you receive reflects your importance. It is not unusual for Joe to receive 100 emails a day. Many are cc's, which he has every intention of reading but rarely does. This has caused embarrassment on several occasions when colleagues assumed Joe to be up to speed on a project.

Joe believes in 'crisp' emails often replying with a simple yes or no. This style often appears brusque to his colleagues, particularly for those in overseas offices. Joe has upset colleagues with what he thought was a short, snappy email but to them seemed rude and aggressive. This effect is amplified by his constant use of upper case and exclamation marks. Joe is too busy for niceties, 'If they don't like it, tough! I haven't got time to pussyfoot about. At least they get a response.' This can cause frustration and resentment from colleagues. On occasions they would really like more information and even detail on what and when they are supposed to be doing something. They would like him to indicate the priority of the work, which he delegates fast and furiously by email. From Joe's point of view, sending emails saves him having to have lots of pointless meetings and long conversations with colleagues and clients. Although he delegates work he prefers to chase and check progress and now he can do this with daily (even hourly) emails. He is not the most trusting of managers and his constant hovering style of management causes a lot of stress in his team.

It is thought that Joe has an 'allergy' to the phone as he far prefers to email or simultaneously 'instant message' his colleagues – his latest way to 'talk' to them and check instantly how they are doing.

Joe rarely goes anywhere without the laptop and is testing a new piece of real time software. This will speed up the process especially when Joe is away on business trips. Over the years Joe has collected a bag full of cables and connections for every eventuality around the world. This goes on every overseas trip – holidays included. Joe's colleagues used to look forward to him being away on business trips or holidays as this gave them some peace. Not any more! Boring meetings, the back of a taxi, trains, airport lounges and holidays lasting more than two days are all an opportunity for Joe to 'zap a few more emails'. When there isn't time to switch on the laptop, he can send a text message. Joe takes pride in an instant response and much to their frustration expects nothing less from colleagues. After all, we live in a 24 hour global economy now!

2.4.2 What is revealed about Joe's executive lifestyle?

Management style

Always in a hurry
Micromanages – likes to know exactly what is going on and uses email to manage
Can create stress for those around him
Places more emphasis on things rather than people
A brusque style of management and communications

Information needs

Likes to feel he has all the key information he needs at his fingertips but rarely uses it
Finds it hard to prioritize and rarely files any emails which makes it hard for him to find old ones
Thinks he is well informed when in reality information overload means he is probably unenlightened

IT fitness

Gold level
A poor role model of email citizenship
Wonders how anyone functioned before the arrival of the PC and email

Communications patterns

Prefers email to most other forms of communications
Likes short sharp communications and has little time for the pleasantries that help create relationships
Gives little thought to how others might interpret what he writes

Work–life balance

Finds it hard to switch off when on leave and email is the perfect foil for him to keep in touch with the office and keep the adrenaline flowing

2.4.3 How could Joe make email add more value to his work life?

Joe's snappy almost 'shooting from the hip' approach to email is symptomatic of his general style of management. First and foremost Joe should start to engage his brain before he sends another email. If needs be, he should place and leave each email in the 'draft box' for at least one hour before he sends it. He should try to limit the number of emails he sends per day and actively seek opportunities to use other methods of communication (e.g. the phone).

This will be hard. Indeed, he might need to go on a management course to help adopt a more planned, people-centred approach to management and communications in general.

He should consider what information he really needs from his colleagues in order to do his job. He should then tell people and ask to be removed from the cc lists of emails he really never reads. He should ask his colleagues to put his name in the 'To' rather than 'cc' address box if action is required from him.

In this way Joe will decrease the noise level and save himself time dealing with email. He will also reduce the risk of unknowingly upsetting others and begin to become better informed about what is really going on around him. It might enhance the professional image his boss has of him and improve his chances of promotion!

2.5 Case history – Justin Watson (high noise/high information)

2.5.1 Justin – just on-line

Justin loves information and all the new technology and gadgets available to him make it easy to get everything he may need. He starts the day by downloading the newspaper onto the latest handheld computer. This makes it easier to read on the train journey to the office and supports the corporate philosophy of the 'paperless office'. (However, he fails miserably in his office and study at home which features piles of printouts and trays full of trade journals still in their plastic wrappers all waiting to be read – one day.) It's no wonder he has little time for reading because as well as his work he is usually testing the latest piece of hardware or a software package for the company.

Justin believes that having the latest information at your fingertips is essential in business. The day begins with a quick scan of the emails that have arrived during the night followed by a check of the market conditions on the web. Interesting emails are forwarded to colleagues and relevant information from the web is sent out to all who may be interested in the first of many emails for the day. Justin thrives on information and has pride in keeping everyone up to date. Sadly many of Justin's emails go unopened as most people in the office are struggling to handle the important ones without the many 'nice to know', but hardly essential, missives from Justin. Still Justin has become the person in the office to forward all requests for information and on-line surveys. However, all of this 'noise' makes Justin's box something of a minefield in which it's very difficult to spot the really important notes.

Justin's office is never empty of people asking for help and advice with their computer and data. The answer is somewhere . . . if only it could be found. Justin tends to keep everything, just in case it might be needed. He spends hours on a very complicated system of filing all his notes but this makes things hard to find. 'Not to worry, I'll email you with the answer later' is the usual response. On average Justin sends and receives 150 emails a day. Emails are always opened immediately which leads to a very disruptive day. Once opened they often get lost in the system, which can delay action for days. He gets frustrated that he is diverted from his real job by all the interruptions and distractions of the email he receives but feels he must attend to them.

Justin rarely has face-to-face meetings, preferring emails and conference calls. He really hasn't got time for meetings, which get in the way of sending and receiving emails and searching the internet for information. He never seems to have enough of the computer and often stays late or takes work home in the evening. This is not a problem as Justin has a fully equipped office at home that is linked into the office network. His work–life balance is not equal and his partner is not impressed.

During the journey home there is time to read the latest market survey report that has been downloaded from an analysts subscription site. Justin often wonders what life would be like without computers. Colleagues often wish Justin would give it a try!

2.5.2 What is revealed about Justin's executive lifestyle?

Management style

Hurried approach
Finds it hard to delegate and say no
Likes to know what is going on and be involved with everyone and everything and so a high percentage of his email are cc'd
Is easily distracted and finds it difficult to concentrate for long periods of time
Does not manage his time well

Information needs

Likes to think he is well informed but finds it hard to prioritize and identify what his real killer information needs are
Unfocused and hoards emails, just in case
Subscribes to lots of e-newsletters, few of which he reads
The real information is often obscured by the noise and as a result in reality Justin can often be unaware of an impending crisis (or opportunity)
Justin will also often miss out on the subtle nuances of a situation which can only be gained from face-to-face or verbal communications

IT fitness

Gold – is seen as the department's local helpdesk
Always intends to be a better email citizen but never quite manages as his desire to deal with his email there and then takes over any good intentions

Communications patterns

Prefers short exchanges
Email is the medium of choice

Work-life balance

Is very rarely out of touch either at home or when on leave. Like Joe, email is his lifeblood and his addiction can cause friction at home

2.5.3 How could Justin make email add more value to his work life?

Justin's first task is to wean himself off email and onto other forms of communication such as meetings and phone calls. An email-free day for Justin might initially cause him great stress but the long-term result would be astounding.

He (like Joe) would find himself able to achieve his real goal of being well briefed and informed about both the business and what is going on in the office. Again he might need to do some deeper personal development on his time management and communications style.

With his high level of IT fitness, he would be well placed to drive forward a push towards better email citizenship: then he really could put his technical expertise to good use. But he will need to manage himself more effectively and ensure his espoused beliefs and behaviours matched those in practice.

2.6 Case history – Ronnie Sutton (low noise/high information)

2.6.1 Ronnie – the responsible email citizen

Ronnie is a high achiever. She believes in being organized and spends the first few minutes of the day planning and ensuring that the team know their key tasks for the day. 'Time spent in planning is rarely wasted' has been one of the guiding phrases in her successful career. She focuses on the important and doesn't get side tracked by trivia. Ronnie has spent a lot of time thinking about the right level of IT support. Determined not to become a slave to the computer and email, systems and protocols have been developed to give Ronnie the appropriate level of access to right information and people.

The office is organized to ensure that the computer does not dominate. Emails are monitored and filters are in place to prevent Ronnie being bombarded with unnecessary information and emails. Ronnie has developed an email policy called 'email by exception' for the team which is keenly enforced. This means all her team are required to:

- tailor their inboxes;
- file or archive non-urgent but essential mail so it doesn't clog the company server or personal inbox;
- think if email is the best medium for the message;
- desist from automatic caching of everyone in the department or team;
- use instant messaging for the 'What time shall we meet?' type of email.

Emails are not sent when a phone call or conversation will achieve the same results. Cc emails are kept to a minimum and colleagues are urged to return emails they are copied in on but have not requested.

Ronnie really believes in face-to-face contact and regularly holds meetings with colleagues and clients. A real effort is made not to hide behind the computer by simply sending and responding to emails. Emails are opened and sent at certain times in the day and only if a vital one is expected will an eye be kept on the screen. This has caused a few raised eyebrows but it's her way of ensuring that emails do not take over. She has seen too many colleagues become slaves to their computers and there's no way it will happen to her. Every email is sent for a specific reason rather than simply 'fired off' and careful thought is given to ensuring that this is the correct medium to use. Staff know that when they receive an email from Ronnie it is worth looking at and giving careful attention to.

Ronnie applies the same rules for filing and organizing information on the computer as has been developed for paper. **Deal, delegate and delete are the simple but effective rules**. The computer like the office is organized, neat and tidy. Information is easily accessed and Ronnie does not waste time searching the computer every time she wants to find something. If it's worth keeping it needs to be properly filed and easily retrieved.

Ronnie believes in the old edict 'ruthless with time, gracious with people' and believes that for many the computer and particularly emails have become a great waster of time.

2.6.2 What is revealed about Ronnie's executive lifestyle?

Management style

Very focused, assertive but not aggressive
Places high emphasis on people
Good at prioritizing and planning
Believes in delegation and empowerment
Creates trust and a calm atmosphere even when there is a storm brewing
Leads by example

Information needs

Knows exactly what are her killer information needs
Information is regarded as an asset to be used judiciously and not sprayed around the company

Emails are regarded as an important source of information and are filed for easy retrieval

Communications patterns

Focused, but has time to develop relationships
Takes care to think before saying/writing something
Tries to use the best medium for the purpose
Places a high value on face-to-face communications and soft non-verbal signals

IT fitness

Silver level user
Role model of the good email citizen
Manages to instil email best practice across her whole division by setting the standard and being the role model

Work–life balance

Believes in staying off-line when on leave or out of normal office hours, but is available if absolutely needed. (This is rare, as her team are used to trusting their own judgement, and each member has defined responsibilities for different aspects of their job in her absence.)

2.6.3 How could Ronnie make email add more value to her work life?

This is more a case of what can we learn from Ronnie as the role model of a good email citizen. Ronnie has moulded her use of email to her preferred executive lifestyle and how she wants the division both to manage information and communicate. Her ability to plan and prioritize means that email does not distract either her or her team from the main task in hand. Just as she would have dealt with her paper in-tray in an orderly fashion, so she deals with her inbox with the same structured approach.

The main danger for Ronnie is keeping track of any new electronic communications technology and making sure she doesn't miss out because others think she is reticent about IT. The raised eyebrows from peers at the way she handles her inbox are probably jealousy.

Underlying Ronnie's approach to how she uses email is her own management style – assertive, challenging, a high flyer – but she knows how to balance her needs against others in order to draw out the best in them (for example, through meetings and talking to them).

2.7 What your inbox says about you – self-assessment exercise

Look at the statements below, and circle the number you feel most accurately mirrors your personal management protocols for using email.

1	I pick the best medium for my message	1	2	3	4	5	I nearly always use email to communicate
2	I craft my email to suit the respondent's needs	1	2	3	4	5	I use the same style for all my emails
3	Generally, I only deal with my email at set times during the day	1	2	3	4	5	I dip in and out of my inbox all day
4	I have a very clear picture of what information I need for my job (my killer information needs)	1	2	3	4	5	I am not really sure what are my killer information needs
5	Even with electronic communications, valid reliable information is like gold dust	1	2	3	4	5	Information is easy to find, especially with the advent of electronic communications
6	My inbox very rarely contains emails which I have not properly read	1	2	3	4	5	My inbox usually contains quite a few emails which I have not properly read
7	Generally I only handle an email once, then I either deal, delete or delegate it to someone	1	2	3	4	5	I often find it hard to decide what to do with an email and find myself re-reading them at least twice
8	When I send an email the recipient always replies	1	2	3	4	5	Many of my emails go unanswered

2.7.1 Interpretation

Total your score for the boxes you have ticked and enter your score below.

8	10		20		30	40

Low noise — **High noise**
High information — **Low information**

8–10 A clear low noise/high information user
11–20 A medium noise/medium information user, moving towards a low noise/high information user
21–30 A high noise/low information user, who could quickly become a high noise/low information user
31–40 Very much a high noise/low information user

2.8 Summary

This chapter should have helped appreciate how your preferred executive lifestyle is influencing how you manage your inbox and hence the ratio of noise to information. It has especially reviewed how your dominant management style, communication preferences, information needs and patterns of working are determining the level of noise and information in your inbox.

You should now have some insight into your strengths and weaknesses as an email user and how you can build on your positive points and work at overcoming the negative aspects of how you use email. Some aspects of how to deal with the stress factor are dealt with in Chapter 7. However, now you should be well on your way to be a more effective email user.

2.8.1 Seven tips for reducing the volume of email by managing yourself more effectively

1 Check that your management style is not leading you to send too many 'just checking on progress' type of email.
2 Manage your most precious asset – your time: try to reduce the number of times you check your inbox for new mail.

3 Only handle an email once – the golden rule is deal, delete or delegate. For emails requiring time to think before replying, deal may simply mean doing just that – thinking.
4 Try to prioritize just what information you really need to do your job.
5 Next time you are sending an email to someone who works near to you go and talk to them instead.
6 Pause before pressing the reply/new mail key and ask yourself if you really need to send that email. If in doubt don't send it.
7 If you log on while on leave ask yourself what would have been the consequence of not dealing with all those emails. Would the outcome have been better or worse if you had waited until you returned to the office?

3 Email IT fitness

What is email IT fitness?
Will improved email IT fitness save me time dealing with my inbox?
Should we all be striving for the same level of email IT fitness?

3.1 Introduction

Having developed a sound strategy to manage the way you use email, the question to ask yourself is 'How can I use the technology to help me implement my strategy?' Today's email software contains plenty of functions designed to help you save time managing your email. For example, automatically insert a sign-off (signature) at the end of an email, use colour to highlight emails from people and sources of importance to you, and rules to filter and prioritize incoming mail. Indeed, to some extent we are spoilt for choice and it is like being let loose in Aladdin's cave. For the technophile this is nirvana. There are just so many tools to experiment with and different ways to view the emails. For those for whom the software is really just a means to an end, the question is which features will help me reduce the time I need to deal with my email and help me spot the emails of high information value.

This chapter is about how to exploit the power of the software to add value to your way of working without becoming too submerged in it and becoming a technology bore. To do this assumes you know what can be done and what is the available functionality of the software. Most software reference books will tell you about the available features but not the benefits of how they could help you. This chapter is designed to help you see how today's email software really can make your life easier by modelling itself on your chosen ways of working. This is a great improvement on the older software that required you to change the way you worked to fit the way the software worked. There are case histories that show how, by adopting the right level of email IT fitness, you can restrict the noise level in your inbox and enable you to extricate the high information ones more easily.

3.2 What is email IT fitness?

We define email IT fitness to be the sum of your confidence and competence to use the appropriate email software:

Email IT fitness = the combination of technical expertise
+ confidence to use the technology

It is not sufficient to know how to use a specific function; you also need to be very comfortable about using the function. For example, many people know that voting buttons can be used to seek opinions and consensus. However, the majority perceive it is all a bit too technical and hard to implement. Like a swimmer, not everyone needs the same level of physical fitness – the level you need will depend on where and for what purpose you want to swim. If you want to swim the Channel you will need more stamina than if you want simply to cruise up and down the lanes in your local gym's swimming pool.

It is the same with technology. If you are surrounded by a team of dedicated staff who deal with your email and are not too bothered about reading them when away from your office, you may only need a minimal level of IT fitness. In contrast if you like to deal with your email first hand, are not in one place for very long, and want to be able to handle your email at any time in any place you need to be a more confident and skilled user.

Confidence comes with the experience. The more you use technology the more confident you will be about what you can do, but also about exploring other ways your email software could help you. Unfortunately, unlike learning to swim, just because you are very proficient with your email software today it doesn't necessarily mean you will always be an expert user. Author and keen golfer John Updike once commented that in golf, those precious swing 'thoughts of the day' decay as rapidly as the half-life of radium. The pace of technology is changing so fast that the same could be said of your IT fitness. If you don't use the software for a while, the chances are the way to do things will have changed with the next version.

3.3 Levels of email IT fitness

There are three levels of email IT fitness, bronze, silver and gold.

Bronze – is the minimum you need just to survive and keep your head above water. It means you can basically reply to incoming emails, forward emails, send new ones and read attachments. If you want to start filing and sorting your emails you need to build up your stamina to reach the silver level.

Silver – this is the level of stamina you need to swim with the tide. At this level you can create an effective filling system for all your emails, change the way you view your inbox to suit your needs, add and change the automatic signature at the end of a new message, create email groups from your contacts, change the subject line when forwarding an email and set an 'out of office' reply.

Gold – this is where you need to be if you need to access your email on the move, often from an alternative device such as a mobile phone or palmtop and with no extra help. You want to be totally self-sufficient 24×7×365 days a year anywhere on planet earth. Moreover, you will probably have some of your incoming email automatically sorted as it arrives in your inbox, including

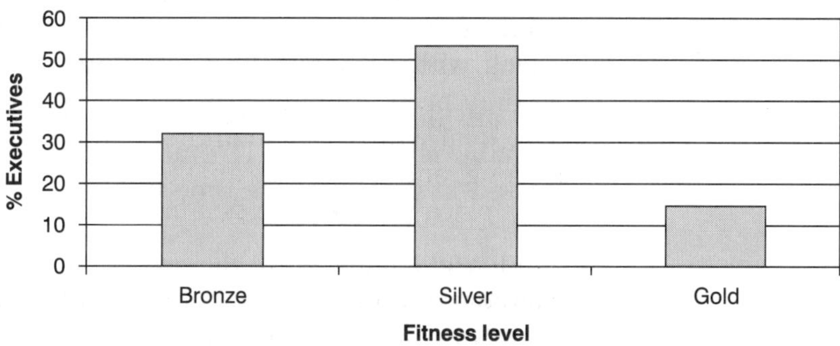

Figure 3.1
Levels of email IT fitness

all types of information in an email from charts to links to web pages and be able to integrate your email with your electronic diary and other personal management tools, e.g. a to-do list.

Figure 3.1 shows a spread of email IT fitness across a group of about 70 typical executives with whom we have worked.

3.3.1 What is right for me?

Like most aspects of management there is no right or wrong. Just because you have achieved the bronze level and your colleague is cruising at gold, it does not mean that either of you is any better. This is not a race to see who can use the most software features in any one email. It is about working at a level of email IT fitness which you are comfortable with and can maintain. What is also important to note is that the level of email IT fitness is independent of:

- job function (e.g. marketing, finance or sales);
- position in the organization;
- size of the organization (from large multinational to independent consultant);
- sector.

It is all about how you want to operate and whether or not you could personally benefit from being more adept with the software. It is also about developing a positive mental attitude towards technology. Bronze users are often the ones who have the least affinity towards technology.

3.3.2 What can I gain from being more proficient with the technology?

First let's be clear about what not to expect when you increase your email IT fitness. Do not expect to reduce the volume of email you receive or the ratio of noise to information. These changes can only be obtained by reviewing how you manage yourself with respect to email and auditing your inbox.

There are three key benefits to be obtained from adopting a reasonable level of email IT fitness. First, you can expect to save time and in particular the time it takes to:

- send new emails;
- forward and reply to emails;
- look for old emails;

- find emails which relate to a meeting you are about to attend;
- stay on top of your to-do list;
- keep track of tasks you delegate to others;
- arrange meetings;
- access your emails when away from the office;
- handle attachments.

Second, being a fitter user will help you highlight the emails of high value and not get distracted by those of low information value and maybe even noise. Third, being more adept with the technology can also help you become a better email citizen and in particular take account of the recipients' preferred working styles.

3.4 Case histories

Here is a typical day in the life of each type of user.

3.4.1 Robert – bronze user

Robert is a group HR director and spends at least two days a week travelling between different office locations. Anne, his PA, initially opens all his email during the week and deals with anything urgent.

Arriving at the office

Robert arrives at his office at 8.45 am just before his first meeting about the new pension scheme. He sees that about ten new emails have arrived overnight. He needs to send emails to Harry the marketing director and Jo the external consultant who is running their time management course next week. He would have liked to catch Arthur in their Beijing office but by now he has gone and Robert is not very good at logging in from home.

Harry is easy as he is on the global company address book. He cannot find Jo's address – it must be there somewhere but he is starting to feel rushed as he still needs to print off the document which arrived late yesterday for today's meeting.

Robert sets the document printing and quickly replies to the email from the CEO. He leaves his secretary to deal with the others. He would have liked to have added his edits to the draft of a document from Gordon he read late yesterday and which they will discuss tonight. He has tried once before but somehow all his changes were lost. So this time he has given his comments to Anne for her to amend and forward to Gordon in time for their meeting tonight.

As he walks out he dictates an email to his PA and hands her the printed copies of yesterday's emails on which he has annotated his replies.

During the meeting

John, the new pension manager, asks Robert if he has the table to hand which he sent him by email yesterday and whether he knew what those working in the Beijing office thought about the scheme. He had copied him in on the dialogue he had with Arthur, but now John needs Robert to talk to Arthur.

Robert had not, as he had been out of the office all day and had only just picked up his email. And he had not yet emailed Arthur. He would ask his PA to do this later. (At this point Robert felt a little marginalized as everyone else seemed to be just a little more in touch with what was going on and almost one step ahead of him.)

After the meeting

It was a long meeting and there were two new people present who needed to be added to the circulation list for this project. He gives Anne the email addresses to add to the list and asks her to forward some old emails that contain relevant information. Robert could do this himself but it would take him a while to find the old emails and the right distribution list (there seem to be so many).

He buys a sandwich for lunch and ploughs his way through the pile of printed emails from the last 24 hours left him by his PA. He scribbles his responses and then scans the five new emails, which have arrived since Anne went for lunch. One he forwards and also sends it to Anne asking her to keep a note to chase up progress in a few days.

He notices a couple of requests for meetings and a note from Sam (a member of his team) asking for approval to attend a conference. He responds to that but decides to leave the diary ones for Anne.

Robert carefully ignores the mounting pile of printouts of older emails. Although he does notice that Anne has now placed them in conventional plastic folders, which are placed in date order on his desk. Robert assumes he will have seen any that are really important and the rest can be skimmed over sometime: maybe on the train this afternoon.

Robert sends one more new email asking for some information and then dashes to catch the train to the Newcastle office.

The end of the day

Robert is staying overnight in Newcastle. He calls Anne to catch up on any late arrivals and dictate a few new ones. Anne will fax through the document, which arrived from the training consultant. Robert for his part will fax Anne his reply in the morning.

Robert ends the day with a working dinner with Gordon, the general manager of the Newcastle office, where they discuss recruitment for the new sales manager and finalize the new flexible working policy for the Newcastle office. Gordon agrees to make the changes and email it to Anne for Anne to send out in Robert's name.

Robert feels that although he gets by dealing with his email, he has a nagging suspicion that he could be saving himself some time if he could at least access his emails from time to time from home (and maybe even another company office like the Newcastle one). That way he could email Anne the letter he is drafting and respond a little more quickly to some of his incoming email, not to mention catching people working in other offices on different time zones.

He has tried to log-on away from the office a few times but it never goes smoothly and he always has to ask for help. And anyway he uses the time he has for other tasks such as drafting reports and catching up on the ever-mounting pile of reading.

What would Robert gain from enhancing his email IT fitness?

There is nothing wrong with how Robert operates, in the sense that he is committing an offence. However, there is no doubt that he could save time dealing with his email if he could access them when away from the office. He would also find he is better informed and able to keep track of dialogues between offices working on different time zones.

In the time it takes him to plough through the paper copies he could have dealt with the bulk of them on the screen rather than go through this three-stage process. (There will always be some emails that need to be printed and thought about before replying.) Robert is probably making double work for his PA who can never be quite sure when he has opened an email, if he has either dealt with it or just scanned it. Together they could develop a system of folders into which they put emails to avoid handling an email twice (see Chapter 8).

He could have emailed the letter he drafted to his PA and again saved them both some time and duplication of effort.

Robert should learn to be more confident using address books and distribution lists. Being able to access his email away from the office would probably help him and make him feel generally more effective. He is not a great lover of technology. There is therefore little chance that he will start to become too absorbed or obsessed with it to the point of losing sight of the real business objective.

His inbox is currently erring towards high noise/high information. Only when he starts to become more of a direct user will he see just how much irrelevant email he is receiving. Then he can start to reduce the noise levels in the ways outlined in Chapter 6. Meanwhile, his PA will have a little more time to finish doing some much needed market research on possible providers for a new in-company senior management programme.

There is always a trade-off for someone like Robert. How much should he interact with his email directly and let this eat into his time and how much should he leave to someone else. Where they can, bronze users more than most have a tendency to be more chauffer driven than perhaps they should be, just because of their relatively low level of IT fitness. Most of the executives we know feel it is better to try to deal with as much as possible yourself. That said, Robert must be careful not to become addicted and should continue to ring fence off time for reading and thinking.

In summary, access to a PC device while away from the office (but not necessarily in transit) would make his life run more smoothly.

3.4.2 Ruth - silver user

Ruth is the marketing director for a medium-sized engineering company. She has a desktop computer in her office and a lightweight laptop for use at home and when she travels, which is about one day a week.

The morning

Ruth is spending the morning working from home on a new marketing campaign. First she checks her inbox and deals with the 15 new emails. Some she replies to and forwards immediately. On one that she forwards she also changes the subject line so that the recipient can quickly see the relevance to him. Then she switches from the company address book to her personal contacts list and sends a note to three people in external organizations with whom she is working on a new public relations campaign for safety in the engineering industry. Ruth also remembers to change her automatic signature from her internal to her external one. The latter contains full contact information (full phone number, mobile number, etc.) rather than just her internal extension number, which is not that helpful to outside people.

Ruth scans the two trade e-newsletters that have come in and spots a piece about their competitors. She forwards this to all those working on the Redtop project using a preset distribution list which ensures they keep ahead of the game. It took her a little time to set up this Redtop distribution list and then she had to modify it when a couple of people said they did not want to receive everything, only exceptional information. Ruth feels this news falls into that category and copies them in on this email.

The rest of the morning

That all takes about half an hour and now Ruth is ready to start working on the new marketing campaign for Redtop. She is on broadband and her email is always on, but now turns off all the functions which tells her when new mail has arrived (pinged and on-screen notices). She edits the project plan contained in an attachment sent to her yesterday. Then she works on an outline brief for their PR agency.

When she has finished both documents she emails them to the Redtop project Steering Committee using another of her distribution lists. At the same time she checks her incoming email. Fifteen new emails in the space of about two hours.

Ruth is involved in several high profile projects. She quickly scans the list to see if there are any relating to 'Timberbox', another hot project. This is one that needs a quick response, and she deals with it there and then. She then prints of a copy to remind herself to follow up on that specific action in a few days' time. She also copies it to her assistant to ask her to undertake a part of the task. She tries to clear all her new emails by the end of each day – including filing them in the relevant folder, and decides to leave the rest until later and prepares to go to an off-site meeting (hoping there is nothing critical).

After the meeting

At 5.30 Ruth returns to her office. There she spends about an hour clearing the remainder of the morning's email plus another 30 emails that have arrived during the afternoon. First, she tries to pick out those which are important for her, and deals with them. Then she just picks her way through the rest, leaving the e-newsletters (marketing pushes) until last. She wishes there was a way of making the emails which relate to certain key projects stand out while at the same time putting her e-newsletters letters into a separate folder.

Gill, the new member of the PR agency, has emailed her some background papers and an electronic business card. Ruth clicks on it to automatically create a new contact in her personal address book. She then replies to Gill and also includes an electronic business card so Gill can do likewise.

She needs to set up a meeting with several members of the Redtop team including some people from their suppliers. She uses voting buttons to gain some idea of which is the most popular date. (For the internal members of the team this is easy as she can check their diaries but this is not an option for the others, and she finds using the voting buttons saves time.)

Ruth is on leave tomorrow. Before she leaves she sets her 'out of office' auto reply that directs anyone to Brian her assistant if they have an urgent query.

Ruth has received about 50 new emails today of which nearly all are of high information content and few noise. About 25 per cent are e-newsletters, which she feels are a valuable way of keeping up with sector and industry specific news. She sent about 15 emails during the day. Over the years she has honed her use of email to make sure she receives only what she needs. She tries to respect other people's working habits and be helpful by making her messages clear (e.g. changing the subject heading when forwarding). Although, she manages to keep on top of her inbox by being fairly disciplined and using the technology reasonably well she has watched others who seem to gain more performance out of the software and make it work a little harder for them.

How would enhancing her email IT fitness help Ruth?

Ruth uses the technology well and does not waste her time or that of her colleagues by playing email ping-pong. She uses her distribution list to target her email and save herself time. She is a good email citizen as she changes the subject line when forwarding an email to make it more obvious why the recipient needs the email.

However, there are two features that would help her manage her inbox even more efficiently, namely, rules and creating an automatic diary entry from an email. She could use rules to organize incoming mail so that it is coloured according to different people/projects, for example red for the Redtop project and brown for Timberbox. She could also use rules to sort and automatically place in folders some of the incoming e-newsletters. They would still show up as new and unread but they would not be cluttering up her main inbox. Not only that, Ruth would not need to sort them into the appropriate folder after she has read them as they are already in the correct folder. This way Ruth would be able to extricate more easily the emails of high value from those of lower priority and in some cases just noise.

Most email software allows you to generate an automatic entry on the calendar task list (for both yourself and those who you work with – assuming you are networked). This means Ruth would not have to ask her assistant to remind her to follow up, as the prompt will appear as a diary reminder. This is really useful for people working on their own or those who do not have access to a dedicated secretary. (Automatically creating an action in someone else's diary or task list might not be so desirable.)

In summary, by increasing her expertise with rules to organize her inbox and learning how to link and create calendar and task list entries automatically, Ruth would boost her level of IT fitness to gold and this will save her between 10 and 20 minutes per day.

3.4.3 Peter – gold user

Peter is the operations director for a large public sector organization. They have two main offices in London and Manchester and three other smaller offices. He has a PA who deals with all diary matters, but he prefers to personally handle his inbox unless he is on leave.

Before leaving home at 6.30 am

Peter checks his email although he is not expecting much as he cleared his inbox at midnight before going to bed. There is one from his counterpart in America to which he replies. At the same time he sends an email to Frank who is in India on a two-week assignment. He is hoping that by now Frank has the data he needs in order to complete the report he is working on. He would like to flag the status of Frank's project at today's board meeting. He quickly synchronizes his palmtop before being driven to the station to catch his train to London.

Peter has installed a network at home as both his wife and children have PCs. They have several email addresses between them (for work and social use). Besides his main PC and a small but powerful laptop, he also has a palmtop. He is only taking his palmtop today as it has all his key documents including the presentation he will give in the morning.

During the journey

With his palmtop he reconnects to his email (by dialling in through his mobile phone) and sends a couple of new ones. At last there is a message from Frank. During the train journey to the London office, Peter continues to work on email and drafting some documents. One email had a large attachment, which was a bit of hassle to download, but he has it now.

He makes a mental note to remind his team not to send him emails with large attachments when he is in transit.

At the London office

At 9.00 am just before the board meeting Peter quickly synchronizes his palmtop with his desktop PC. Slowly the world is waking up and there are ten new emails including three e-newsletters. He is involved in several projects, which are on the critical path. He has used rules and specifically colours to organize his inbox. For example, all incoming email relating to the installation of the new network is in purple. He spots the one from James telling him there were no problems last night with the trial run and none this morning.

There is a copy of a press release that he needs to clear. He edits the document and sends it back to the communications department. There are two invitations to events. He annotates and forwards these to Pam his PA who deals with the diary to check that he can attend and make the necessary travel arrangements.

The three e-newsletters have automatically gone into folders for him to read later. Just time to fire off a couple more emails about the new data Frank has sent him. By 10.00 am he has dealt with about 20 incoming emails and sent about the same number.

During the board meeting Peter takes notes on his palmtop. There is a working lunch and he is careful not to be seduced into checking his email. It can all wait for another hour.

After the meeting

After the meeting he spends about ten minutes tidying up his notes and generating a Word document from the electronic file, which he initially created on the palmtop. Peter then circulates the minutes to the other board members. He extracts the action points and circulates them to his team. He has several distribution lists so this only takes a minute. Finally, he generates an automatic reminder (on his calendar and task list) for him to follow up on certain points.

Later that afternoon

It is now about 4.00 pm and he spends the next half an hour dealing with his inbox which now contains about 30 new emails, of which about half are copied to him rather than addressed to him directly. He doesn't receive too much spam as the organization has software to stop the bulk of it getting through. But he is still getting some from odd mailing lists. Even at home he has installed firewall and anti-spam software.

Then he catches up with his PA and they talk through arrangements for the rest of the day. Peter likes handling his own email although several other members of the board use their PAs to filter it. He finds it quicker to handle his own, but is careful to copy his PA in on anything she needs to be aware of such as meetings.

He uses his instant messaging software to alert Carol, who he's about to meet, that he will be about ten minutes late. He also sends an instant message to Paula, the IT manager, to forewarn her that the finance director wants to talk about budgets later in the day. Peter emails George who works in another office to see if he wants to meet for an early evening drink tonight. He sets an expiry date of tomorrow on the email: if George is away the email is redundant so there is no need for it to sit clogging up his inbox.

Before he leaves, Peter does a little more work on the report he has been working on all week. He has it as a shortcut on his Outlook Shortcut bar. This means he can access it directly from within the Outlook email software with one click of the mouse.

At 7.30 pm he goes to meet a supplier for dinner. When he returns to his hotel he quickly rechecks his inbox through his palmtop and mobile phone and sends an email to James with a note of the conversation he had with the supplier.

Could Peter use the technology to handle his email any more effectively?

Probably not. Peter receives about 70 emails a day and up to 100 on a bad day. His inbox certainly contains a high level of information and it may be verging on the border of high noise. However, he is using rules to organize the incoming email to target those with high information content.

Like many gold users Peter needs to make sure that he does not start becoming obsessed with the technology and sending emails when a phone call or meeting would be better. He might think about the impact of sending email late at night and very early in the morning. Although this suits his style of working it can be stressful for others. He could use the timing function to preset a more friendly time to have the email sent. This would heighten his profile as a good email citizen.

Otherwise, Peter is probably obtaining a very good return on his investment in his IT fitness programme. Being a gold user means he is exploiting the full power of the available software to support his preferred executive lifestyle and way of working. He has tailored the front page (entry screen) of the email software to allow him access to other files and applications he frequently uses. This again helps him save time, especially coming in and out of different applications. (We are only talking seconds, but as a heavy user of the PC these seconds soon add up during the day.)

He has tried some of the newer always-on email systems (like Blackberry) but prefers the palmtop connected via a mobile, it gives him more functionality and freedom. Although he plans to revisit these new devices again when they have more functionality and are cheaper.

3.5 Bronze to gold – key differences

In addition to sheer technical expertise there are some other subtle, more qualitative differences between the different user types. These relate mainly to:

- the level to which they involve the PA in handling their inbox;
- their interest in technology;
- how they adapt their use of email to accommodate others.

3.5.1 Level of involvement with the inbox

Typically, as indicated above and shown in Figure 3.2, bronze users make limited direct personal use of email. Their secretary or PA will act as the initial filter.

To some extent it is a chicken and egg situation. Their limited confidence and competence with the software means they will often shy away from using email themselves. This does not mean that they will use an alternative medium. It is more about their general disregard for email. They will often have neat piles of unread printed messages just like Robert in the case history. In today's business environment where you often need to be able to communicate outside the normal working hours many bronze users often find they do need to be moving into the silver league. There is no definitive right or wrong.

Indeed, it is not uncommon for a silver user to have their PA handle their inbox while they are busy or in meetings. However, the difference between them and their bronze counterparts is that they can very quickly deal with their email when they need to. It is rare for a gold user to delegate responsibility for their inbox. In part this may reflect their need to remain in control.

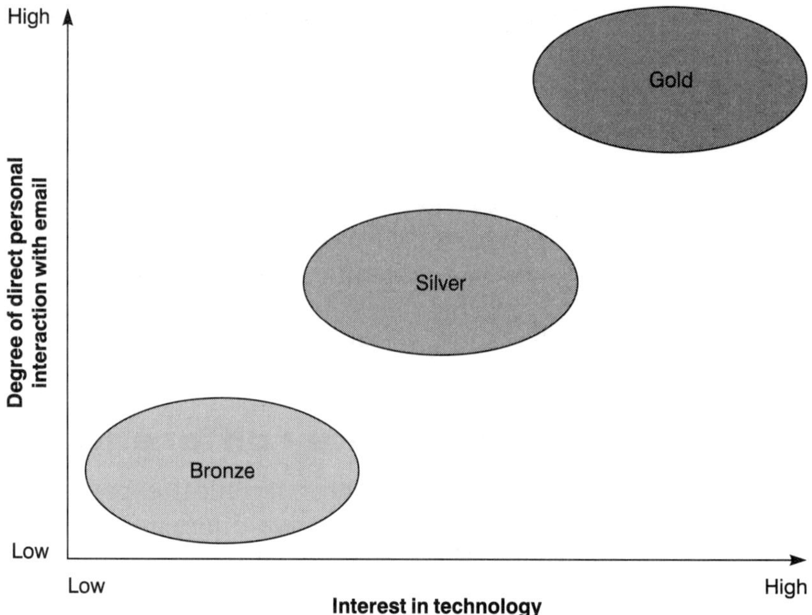

Figure 3.2
Other email IT fitness characteristics

3.5.2 Interest in technology

Not surprisingly and in keeping with general findings on IT fitness, bronze users tend to be the least interested in technology. They use it because they have to and only in so far as it does the job. The notion of exploring just what can be done with the technology leaves them cold. Indeed they would probably rather have a cold shower than try to find out how to link an email to a diary entry. They just don't grasp what could be gained from being more proficient with the technology.

3.5.3 Sensitive use of email

Gold users are often the least sensitive to other people's needs in terms of firing off emails at all times of the night and day. Their use of email is again very much in your face. It is their way of keeping busy, getting things done quickly at all costs. Whereas silver users are often more considerate and will delay sending a message if it is wildly outside the normal working day. It doesn't have to be like that. Gold users with all their expertise could use the software to soften their image.

For example, Joyce is a divisional manager in a government agency. Joyce has three young children and works flexible hours which for her are 5.30 am to 3.30 pm and then maybe for a couple of hours after dinner. But rather than send emails that early in the morning she uses the delayed time function, especially when they are to her team. She feels this is less intimidating and means she doesn't have to impose her working patterns on others.

Sadly, gold users are also more likely to use email even when it is an inappropriate medium. They are also the types that play email ping-pong.

3.6 Summary

This chapter has discussed how you can use the email software to work smarter and save yourself time. The optimum level of email IT fitness will depend on your circumstances. Certainly we don't all need to achieve full gold medal status for email IT fitness. The ideal level is top end of the silver to low end of gold. The technology is there to help you. The key message is:

- For expert users, make sure you do not loose yourself in the technology at the expense of the task in hand.
- For less expert users check that you are not taking too long to execute simple tasks when there may be a quick time saving feature of which you are not aware.

If you have tuned up your personal management techniques then you should be able to save yourself a little more time by boosting your level of email IT fitness.

4 Assessing your email IT fitness

Which functions of my email software can I use really confidently?
What is my current email IT fitness?
Where are the gaps?

4.1 Introduction

In Chapter 3 we saw how you can use your email software to reduce the time it takes to deal with your inbox by simplifying some key tasks such as sending one email to several people and automatically inserting a signature at the end of an email. We also saw how by increasing your level of email IT fitness you can more easily identify those emails, which are of high information value to you. This chapter will enable you to benchmark your personal level of email IT fitness and identify gaps in your expertise.

4.2 The email IT fitness checklist

On the following pages you will find a checklist of tasks commonly associated with specific levels of email IT fitness. Work your way through each section and tick the box that most closely corresponds to how comfortable you feel carrying out that task. It is based on the Microsoft Outlook software and assumes you are working in a corporate network environment. Most software packages have almost identical functionality although the terminology may be different. These nuances are discussed later.

4.2.1 Bronze email IT fitness

Task/Feature	Level of comfort		
	Very comfortable	Comfortable	Need to learn
Access your email system from: • your office desktop PC			
Store contact information: • insert new contact information in the default 'contact' address file			
Compose and send emails: • create new email • insert meaningful subject line • use the contacts address book • input text message • use the spell checker • attach a file (e.g. Word document) • send an email to one person • send an email to a group of people			
Receive incoming emails: • open and read incoming email • reply to incoming email • forward email open files attached to an email, e.g. Word documents			
Manage the inbox: • create folders for filing emails • file emails • save attachments • sort emails into preferred sequence, e.g. by date, name • delete emails			
Respond to email: • reply to sender only • use reply to all where appropriate • forward email to one person forward email to a group of people			

4.2.2 Silver email IT fitness

In addition to the bronze level task, be able to do the following:

Task/Feature	Level of comfort		
	Very comfortable	Comfortable	Need to learn
Access your email system remotely when away from your office, e.g. from a laptop to: • receive incoming mail • send mail			
Contacts files/address books: • create and use other contact lists • create a new contact from a business card (vcf) attached to an email			
Customize email messages: • create customized signatures • automatically insert a virtual business card • create and use templates			
Voting buttons: • use voting buttons			
Auto reply: • create an out of office message • vary your out of office message			
Manage the inbox: • print a list of emails in a folder • change the way emails are viewed • find a current email • archive old emails • retrieve archived emails • keep your inbox within the specified corporate limits (where appropriate)			
Compose and send emails: • send email directly from within other applications, e.g. Word • use bullet points • change the text layout • use receipts			
Work with others with email: • forward email and edit subject line • forward email and edit text of message			
Virus protection: • recognize potentially infected emails • delete potentially infected emails			

4.2.3 Gold email IT fitness

In addition to the bronze and silver level, be able to perform the following time saving tasks:

Task/Feature	Level of comfort		
	Very comfortable	Comfortable	Need to learn
Customize your email software: • customize the entry front page to suit personal use • add shortcuts to access other frequently used applications from within the email software			
Create email messages: • creating links to files in shared network drives • insert information in another application directly into an email (e.g. a chart) • insert hyperlinks to websites			
Manage emails: • create shared folders • change colour used to highlight unread emails • change fonts and colour used for editing • use 'rules' and 'organize' automatically to sort emails • move an email between different parts of the software, e.g. to create tasks and calendar entry			
Send emails: • time sending emails, e.g. delay to suit work patterns of others or send when away • insert an 'expiry date' after which the email self-deletes in the recipient's inbox • automatically ask for a reply from a recipient			
Edit internet connections: • add new internet connections • edit existing connections (e.g. change the access phone number and password)			
Work with anti-virus software: • customize the software, e.g. to run regular updates			

4.3 Scoring

To achieve full membership of any one specific level of IT fitness, you should be 'very comfortable' undertaking at least half of any of the stated tasks. If you are only 'comfortable' with about half the tasks, this indicates that you need some help to achieve that level of IT fitness.

A bronze to silver level user – you are very comfortable with at least half those tasks associated with the bronze league but less than half in the silver league and only a couple in the gold league. You are probably just a silver level user. To really merit a silver medal you should learn how to expedite at least half of the silver user tasks.

A full silver medalist – you would be very comfortable undertaking all the tasks listed for a bronze user and over half those listed for a silver user.

A silver to gold user – you would be very comfortable not only with all the tasks in the bronze and silver users' list but also about six or seven of those listed for the gold user.

A gold medalist – you will be familiar with all the tasks listed in both the bronze and silver level users and over half those on the gold user list.

You don't have to use all the features to qualify for full membership of a specific division and indeed some may not add any value for you (e.g. colour coding). However, the defining criterion is that you can use them when you need to. In essence it is about identifying what you don't know and then learning how to use those functions as and when they can add value to how you want to work.

> My current level of email IT fitness:
>
> My ideal level of email IT fitness would be:
>
> Do you feel this is right for you? If not, this exercise should have helped you identify where you could improve in order to make the software work more efficiently for you.

4.4 Nuances and subtleties across different environments

There are some subtle differences between the different email packages such as Notes, Outlook, Eudora, Pegasus and Entourage (for Apple Mac users). For example, the main differences between Notes and Outlook are summarized in Table 4.1.

Table 4.1 Differences between Notes and Outlook

Function	Notes	Outlook
Shortcuts to other applications		'Shortcut Bar' is specially designed for Outlook.
Replicating your local PC with the corporate file server	Known as 'Replication' in Notes and is unique to Notes.	No comparable feature within Outlook.
Customizing the front page	In the latest version of Notes (version 5) you can customize the front page and bookmark where you want to go, e.g. Notes databases, or specific document.	Outlook lets you customize the entry screen; for example, you can just go directly to your email, or your diary.
Templates and letterheads	Notes provides a range of pre-formatted letterheads and templates, and also a 'mood stamp'. The latter is designed to let you add some feeling to your email, e.g. a smiley for a thank you.	You can create templates but there is no 'mood stamp' option.
Rules to organize the inbox	You can only use rules automatically to move new email to folders. There is no facility to colour code incoming email.	You can create rules to manage the incoming email by folder and by colour.
Bulletin Boards	These again are unique to Notes and designed to allow you to share information through common databases.	Not available in Outlook.

These are the main differences and largely highlight the fact that Notes is the true form of knowledge sharing groupware, designed for one to many communications. This is reflected in the bulletin board infrastructure. This book is not the place to argue the case for or against either system. This is a decision that will need to be made in conjunction with your IT department who will be able to provide you with more information.

4.4.1 Folders and email IT fitness

Perhaps one of the greyest areas of email IT fitness is the use of folders. We are often asked whether or not everyone should put their emails into folders.

The rational ones among us will say yes. If they are in folders it will be easier to find. However, some people find it just as quick to scroll through screens of unsorted email. Take this example of Steve, UK managing director of a medium-sized multinational software company:

> *I treat my inbox like I treated my bedroom as a teenager. Everything is piled up but I know exactly where my things are. If someone tidies it up, I can't find anything. But there comes a point when I just have a blitz and throw out all the junk.*

Steve is a silver user who uses both email and text messaging but hates spending time filing until he absolutely must. His inbox is in date order and he will happily work with several hundred in his inbox at any one time. When he does tidy up the emails they go in one of four folders – personnel, marketing, clients or cash/flow.

Contrast this with Jackie who is the founding managing partner of medium-sized international PR agency:

> *I like to keep myself organized and try to keep the number of unsorted emails in my inbox and sent items to ten. Everything (received and sent email) is filed by projects. Our company best practice policy encourages creating files by client names. This makes it easier for others to find things when you are away.*

Jackie meticulously files her email once she has read it and will sometimes file one email in several places where it relates to multiple projects or people. She is also diligent about clearing out old emails especially those that are part of a dialogue: she deletes the old emails and only saves the last one.

4.4.2 Out of office reply

It's funny, we all have some sort of 'not available message' on our phone but are less reluctant to do this with email. Like many functions you can have several template (predefined) messages and then all you need to do is activate the right one. For example:

> *I am out of the office today. If it is urgent please call.*
>
> *I am in a meeting from 8.30 am until 12.30 pm and will deal with all my email on my return.*

Those not working in a corporate network environment (e.g. independent consultant, sole trader, etc.) may be denied this facility: although some ISPs can provide the function. It is also one of the benefits of broadband.

4.5 Summary

This chapter should have helped you assess your current level of email IT fitness. It will have highlighted any obvious gaps in your competence and shown you how to make your email software work harder for you. Here are ten sure ways you can use your email software to reduce the time you spend handling your email. These fall into two categories, those designed to reduce the time it takes to send email, and those that diminish the noise element and enable you identify the high information ones more readily. Just because someone else might think his or her email is important you may not want it clogging up your radar screen of the world.

4.5.1 Ten ways to let the software handle your email more smartly

Saving time sending email

1 Create an automatic signature (sign-off).
2 Use distribution lists (groups) for sending one email to many people.
3 Use 'voting buttons' (or the equivalent feature) to gain consensus, e.g. for a meeting or agreement to a suggestion. (In Notes you can do this through the shared calendar feature or for gaining consensus to a discussion through the 'Discussion Threads' folder.)
4 Set an out of office reply when you are away, even if it is only for a short time.
5 Create shortcuts from your email software to key applications and files that you use frequently.

Diminishing the noise and highlighting the information

1 Create rules to filter automatically non-essential email (e.g. newsletters) – this will help you reduce the noise element of your inbox.
2 Colour-code incoming email – this will help you identify the emails that are important to you.
3 Tailor how you view your emails to suit you (e.g. a list or a split screen with a preview of the whole email).
4 Use folders to store both sent and received email.
5 Link time critical emails to your calendar or task list so you can keep track of them and have them to hand when needed.

5 Boosting your email IT fitness

How can I boost my email IT fitness?
How long will it take me to reach peak performance?
How can I maintain my chosen level of email IT fitness?

5.1 Introduction

IT fitness like physical fitness is about your physical expertise (in this case technical competence) and mental attitude. Perhaps you have little or no interest in computers. You may even dislike or have a negative attitude towards them. Alternatively, you may love your computer but not have time to learn how to unleash its full potential. Whether or not you like email, it is the *Zeitgeist* of today's business and to some extent social world. With email traffic predicted to grow to over 36 billion by 2005, the best learning investment you could make over the next few months would be to boost your level of email IT fitness. That means increasing your overall confidence as a user and your technical prowess. As you know, top sports people have a good mental attitude. However, to succeed they also have to have well-developed technical skills and this means constantly honing and developing their abilities. This could be said to apply equally to using email.

This chapter provides some ideas on how to develop and maintain your personal email IT fitness (issues relating to corporate levels of email IT fitness are addressed in Chapter 16). Like most aspects of life our ability to perform is often influenced by our own preconceptions, in this case about IT in general. This chapter includes an exercise for you to gauge your current disposition towards information technology, some suggestions about how to learn to love your computer, and how to maximize its potential.

5.2 The game plan

Improving and maintaining your email IT fitness is a simple five-stage process as shown in Figure 5.1. First and foremost you need a learning strategy designed to help you achieve your

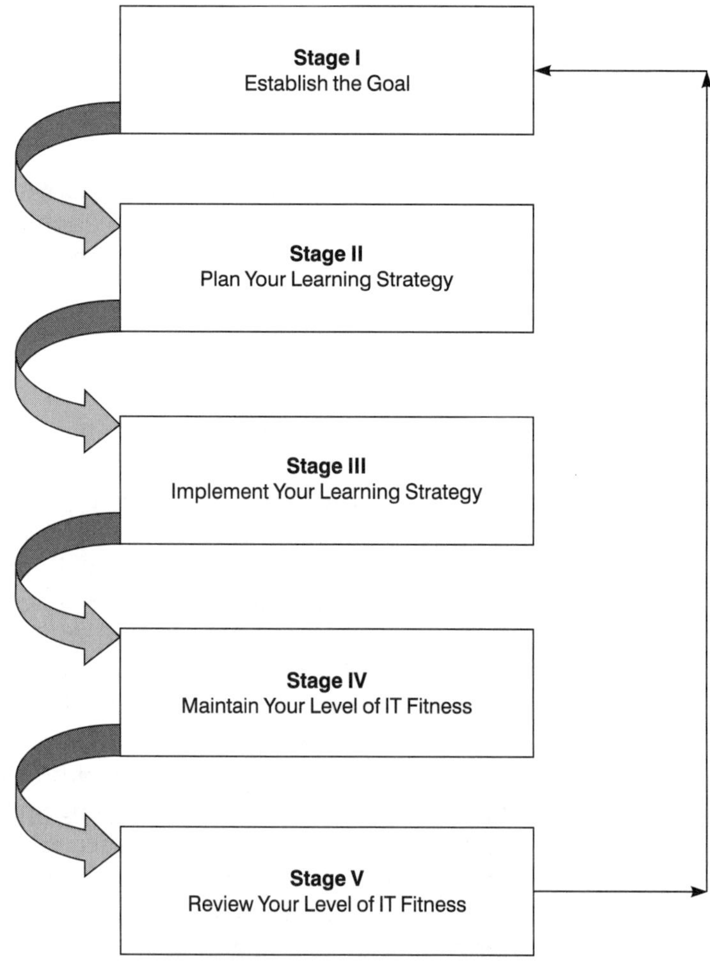

Figure 5.1
Improving and sustaining your email IT fitness

goals. This means benchmarking your current level of email IT fitness and deciding on the level you are aiming for.

5.2.1 Stage I – Set yourself SMART goals – this is key to success

Specific and precise targets (e.g. move to the silver level).
Measurable – a criterion by which you will know you have achieved your goal.
Achievable – challenging but not beyond your reach.
Relevant – to what you do and your available resources.
Timely – a realistic timeframe.

For example, you might be a bronze user whose inbox is 50 per cent noise. A SMART goal would be to achieve silver level email IT fitness within say a month, and within three months reduce the level of noise to 25 per cent.

5.2.2 Stage II – Plan your learning strategy

Decide how, where and when you will improve your email IT fitness. In Section 5.3 we outline some of the available sources of help.

5.2.3 Stage III – Implement your plan

It is surprising how many other urgent projects, meetings and activities can overshadow your development plan unless you are really committed to it. This is especially the case for those with a slightly negative predisposition towards technology. One way to prevent this is to make your email IT fitness programme a high priority. If you have a secretary ask her to preserve the time you have scheduled for your personal development programme. Don't let someone else highjack this precious time – this is your time for you.

How long it will take you to reach your target will depend on:

- the gap between your current and planned level of email IT fitness;
- how you choose to learn;
- how often you use your system and hence how much time you have to practice.

Those who make the quickest progress are not necessarily those who have the most positive attitude towards technology. Rather they are those who are prepared to make the time to use their newly acquired skills, as often as possible as illustrated by the two case histories at the end of this section.

5.2.4 Stage IV – Maintain your level of email IT fitness

As the technology landscape is forever shifting you must be prepared to see and accept learning to use technology as a lifelong learning process. Expertise hard earned today may be redundant in six to 12 months as the software and available email devices become ever more intelligent and sophisticated. Suggestions about how to sustain fitness are discussed in subsequent sections.

5.2.5 Stage V – Review your level of email IT fitness and the goals you first established

Ask yourself if they are still appropriate and correct for you. Maybe you initially set a target of becoming a silver user and reducing the level of noise by 20 per cent. Now you have achieved that goal and become more confident and self-sufficient it might be conceivable to move toward gold and reduce the noise by a further 10 per cent.

5.2.6 Case histories

John, chief executive of a leading defence organization, was just a bronze user who only interacted directly with his email once or twice a week, as a secretary mainly dealt with his inbox. John decided to have a series of one-to one coaching sessions. He had little time to practise between sessions as he spent much of his time in meetings either in his office or away. Although, when he was in, his PA actively encouraged him and helped him to use his email. She also arranged for him to have a laptop at home. It took him about six to eight weeks to move to the low end of the silver division. As he became more adept he started to use his email more often and after about another six weeks was very comfortable handling his own inbox both in the office and at home.

Penny, director of a division of a government agency, was a low-end silver user who primarily dealt with her own email but had a secretary who handled the inbox when Penny was in meetings. Penny decided to achieve gold status. She had two one-to-one IT fitness coaching sessions and within two weeks was operating at the gold level, saving herself time and acting as a better email citizen.

5.3 Sources of help

There are a number of ways you can boost your email IT fitness which include:

- attending courses;
- one-to-one IT fitness coaching;
- software built-in help;
- e-learning (self-teaching packages);
- computer books and magazines;
- websites;
- other users.

In the following subsections we review the advantages and disadvantages of each source and when one might be more appropriate than the other.

5.3.1 Courses

We have probably all been on a course at some stage in our career so there is little more to say here. Just make sure that if you want to go on a conventional instructor led course, the one you book is exactly that. Some activities billed as courses are in fact merely e-learning (computer-based training). All you are doing is paying for the pleasure of going to another location and drinking their coffee rather than sitting beside your own PC. Although there are the motivation and distraction factors, which are a bonus, when you go away from your office for training.

The main advantage is that it makes you commit and focus. The principal disadvantages are matching your availability and needs to those of the course. There is nothing more frustrating than attending a course and finding everyone is on a different plain to you, either streaks ahead in terms of their IT fitness or miles behind.

5.3.2 One-to-one IT fitness coaching

This is conventional coaching but focused on helping you manage your email better. The main advantage is that every session should be geared specifically to your needs and your business environment. You can use the email IT fitness checklist to enable your IT fitness coach to home in on the gaps. Sessions can also be arranged to dovetail into your personal schedule. Sixty to 90 minute one-to-one sessions are a very effective way for managers to boost their email IT fitness as highlighted by this quote:

> *[Coaching has] proved invaluable in enabling me to climb up the learning curve, master the essentials of email and text generation and operate effectively. It has improved my strike rate.*
>
> Stephen, senior advisor to a government organization

Most people find that after 90 minutes their mind starts to wander and their eyes glaze over. This is especially true when learning to use computers. So, even if you are attending a class or working your way through a self-teaching e-learning package, make sure you take a break after about 90 minutes.

5.3.3 E-learning programs

Again many of you will be familiar with these either as e-learning or more conventional computer-based training packages. For every good e-learning package there are probably five poor ones. Poor in the sense that they do not provide adequate feedback, the content is a little trivial, it talks down to you, and the content is not well structured.

That said most organizations these days provide some form of e-learning programs on IT related subjects such as how to use your email software.

The best e-learning programs are those which provide some form of dedicated tutorial help whether on-line or at the place where you are using the program. For a whole course on how to use your email software, this might be a selection criterion for the program you choose. Whereas for a keyboard training package this might be overkill.

The key to using e-learning is to recognize that you need to be motivated to complete the course. How good are you at learning on your own? Do you have a natural affinity for technology? Do you have a history of starting self-teaching programs but never finishing them? If so, e-learning might not be for you, and especially if you are not that enthusiastic about computers and technology *per se*. You would probably be more successful with a course or one-to-one coaching.

5.3.4 Software help function

The built-in help, which comes with most software (and especially Microsoft products), has improved markedly over the years. It generally comes with a set of easy-to-follow instructions on how to execute the task you have looked up: you are guided to the right menu, which option to pick and then which submenu and so on, until the task is complete. (Indeed the latest versions of the Microsoft products have 'wizards' which guide you through the steps of complex functions (e.g. rules).)

Even those of us who are experienced users forget how to use a function from time to time and need to turn to the help function. Accessing the built-in help can be done through several ways such as:

- F1 key;
- 'Help' icon on the main toolbar;
- via the 'Office Assistant' (for Microsoft products).

If you are working with Microsoft products don't feel inhibited and shy about having the 'Office Assistant'. It is a really useful adjunct to any other learning activities and it may even make you laugh, as some of the images are really very humorous. The Office Assistant is rather like an old fashioned servant (or Jim Hacker from *Yes Minister*). It is loyal and will never let you falter without offering advice about what to do next. Alternatively, it can be programmed to speak only when spoken to, for example when you type in a question.

Some organizations also provide their own help databases of frequently asked questions (FAQs). These too can be a mine of useful tips and hints. It is always amazing how few people are aware of these valuable in-house resources.

5.3.5 Websites

Again, the producer of your email software will have a dedicated website with numerous tips and hints often culled from users just like you. These too can be a very useful source of learning.

5.3.6 Computer books and magazines

Neither of the authors are what you might call typical nerds. Yet perusing popular weekly and monthly computer magazines like the 'doorstoppers' available in most high street newsagents and the national newspaper technology sections often reveals a handy time-saving tip or interesting website. There are also some very good self-help books such as the 'Dummies Guides' and 'Teach Yourself Visually' series (see the Bibliography).

5.3.7 Other users

Find someone who is good with IT, whom you respect and let them become your role model. Talk to them, ask them how they use the technology, explain the type of tasks you want to do and ask them if they would show you how they would do it. Imitation is the surest form of flattery and you will quickly find you have your own personal helpdesk. Role modelling is a well-respected and proven way of learning regardless of the topic and it works just as well for IT as Jack Welch (2001) found. Welch learned to use a PC quite late in his business career. He then insisted all his senior managers found themselves an 'IT mentor' (often a whiz-kid 20 years their junior), to learn about the business potential of the internet and electronic communications.

Whatever the final outcome of the dotcom era the principle of the role model remains the same. Many is the time an executive has come to us for help because he has been observing how his peers use their PC and wants to do the same.

The main downsides of role modelling for IT fitness is that your role model might be a technocrat who speaks in too much jargon and finds it hard to explain in simple steps what to do. For the expert user, it is very easy to forget that all-important keystroke, which is second nature to them, but not for the uninitiated (e.g. a double click of the left mouse button). There is also availability and time. The person you choose might not be around when you most need some help.

5.4 Picking the right resource for me

This is a brief overview of the different ways the managers we know have successfully developed their email IT fitness. One of the attributes of Microsoft products is the numerous different ways which you can do something, e.g. send a new email. The more you read and talk to other users the more of these little tricks you can learn. There is never just one right way to do something in a Microsoft environment. It's about finding a way which suits how you use your PC and which you can remember.

By trying different learning approaches and resources you can quickly widen your repertoire of nifty ways to do things. (For example, moving certain incoming email to a folder can be done either through the 'Organize' button on the main toolbar or through the 'Rules Wizard' on the Tools menu. If you are working in Word you don't have to exit to send a new email, there is a 'new email' icon on the Word toolbar which will take you straight there.)

Which of these many resources you find to be of value will depend on a number of factors such as your:

- current level of IT fitness;
- perceptions and attitude towards technology;
- preferred learning style;
- available time.

For example, some managers' dominant learning style is one of discovery and finding things out for themselves: they are well suited to self-teaching packages whether electronic or paper-based in the form of a book. Regardless of their previous experience and level of IT fitness they will happily work things out for themselves. On the other hand you may prefer to be 'told' or taught more directly and be harbouring some doubts about your personal affinity for technology. If this is you, then a course of one-to-one coaching might be a better starting place.

5.5 The winning email IT fitness mind

Unless you are a gold user the chances are that you have some hang-ups about IT in general. You will be harbouring some grudges and negative thoughts probably based on past experiences with computers. For example, the day you lost all your files, the presentation that did not work on someone else's PC, the important email that went missing. These will no doubt be colouring your confidence as to how well you will be able to boost your email IT fitness. Conversely, your enthusiasm for technology might be a weakness for you as an email user. You may be in danger of becoming obsessed with email to the exclusion of other forms of communication. Use the following self-assessment exercise to benchmark your IT awareness and confidence.

5.6 The winning IT fitness mind – self-assessment exercise

Look at the statements below, and circle the number you feel most accurately equates to your attitude towards IT in general. Try not to opt for too many 3s.

1	PCs are fun to use	1	2	3	4	5	PCs are a hassle
2	The benefits gained from using a PC outweigh the investment in my time learning to use one	1	2	3	4	5	The effort to learn to use a PC outweighs the benefits I gain from using one
3	I use my PC whenever I can	1	2	3	4	5	I only use my PC when I really have to and there is no alternative
4	I am very interested in technology as a whole	1	2	3	4	5	Technology doesn't interest me at all
5	It is easy for me to keep pace with technology	1	2	3	4	5	Technology is changing so fast it is very hard to keep pace with the changes
6	It is quite easy for me to learn to use a new piece of software	1	2	3	4	5	I find it hard to learn to use new software
7	Having reasonably good keyboard skills make it easier for me to use a PC	1	2	3	4	5	I can get by with limited keyboard skills
8	I always try to make sure that my use of the PC does not obscure the real task I am working on	1	2	3	4	5	I find it easy to get seduced by the technology and can lose sight of the real task in hand
9	If I am stuck trying to solve a PC related problem I can often sort it myself	1	2	3	4	5	If I am stuck with a PC related problem, I usually need to ask for help
10	I am always on the lookout for new ways to improve my IT fitness	1	2	3	4	5	My level of IT fitness has remained the same for some time

5.6.1 Interpretation

Total your score for the boxes you have ticked and enter your score below.

10		20		30		40		50
Very positive		**Positive**		**Neutral**		**Negative**		**Very negative**

10–19 You are a committed and enthusiastic PC user
20–29 You accept the PC as part of working life
30–39 You only use a PC when you really must
40–50 You actively try to avoid using a PC

Look at the statements where you have scored yourself with a three or more and reflect on how you could overcome some of these negative thoughts and train your mind to visualize using a PC in a more positive light. Below are some specific tips and hints related to your score.

10 to 19 – You are a committed and enthusiastic user of IT and especially PC related devises. Your main concern should be to make sure your use of IT does not overshadow completing the real task in hand. You should have no trouble squeezing the last drop of productivity out of any email software and related tools (e.g. electronic calendar).

You are probably already a gold level user and are just looking at making some minor adjustments to your email IT fitness. You could do this by talking to other expert users (both end users and members of the IT department), looking at appropriate supplier websites, reading popular computer magazines, using self-teaching programs, dipping into the on-line help and maybe even a reference manual.

20 to 29 – You accept the PC as part of your working life and appreciate that it does make a contribution to it (and maybe even your work–life balance). You have a reasonably positive attitude towards using a PC, although you may not have any great affinity towards technology as a whole. You will probably be a mid- to top-end silver user. For you, the best approach to enhancing your level of email IT fitness would be either to attend a workshop with plenty of instructor input or have some one-to-one IT fitness coaching. You might try the on-line help and be pleasantly surprised at your own ability, and this would certainly act as a confidence booster.

30 to 39 – You use a PC because you have to and feel that you should use one, but are probably not very comfortable doing so. PC related tasks probably take you a little longer than they should. Upgrades and new software are perceived as a nuisance, just another thing to distract your attention and time away from the real work of the day. Your email IT fitness is between bronze and low-end silver. No one is saying that we should all love our PCs but feeling that they are more friend than foe will certainly help you when you decide to improve your level of email IT fitness.

A good approach would be to start with some one-to-one IT fitness coaching or attending some classes. Find yourself a role model and ask them for some help. Try reading a little more about the use of IT as a personal management tool (such as those listed in the Bibliography). They are not all laden with jargon and those such as the 'Dummies' series, contain invaluable tips and hints.

Another way to heighten your awareness is to involve yourself in an IT project. This way you can also have some input, create ownership and perhaps provide some often much needed end-user guidance. Many IT departments are crying out for more involvement from users and especially input about how you as a user envisage the software being used.

40 to 50 – *S*omehow you and technology just don't mix and you probably wish for the good old days of pen and ink. The thought of using a PC conjures up dark clouds of doom and gloom. Email doesn't mean there is no place for a conventional letter or scribbled memo, but it is the *Zeitgeist* of today's world of work (and in some cases social networking). You have probably had a few brushes with technology and somehow it always ends in tears. You always feel like you have wasted valuable time when there are others more able than you to do the task.

You are most likely a low-end bronze level user and what you need to do is gain some quick wins. Overwrite the negative experiences with positive ones. The most effective way for you is probably through some dedicated one-to-one IT fitness coaching. This will quickly help you climb the ladder to the top of the bronze division and then into silver. You will be amazed at just how easy it can be with the right coach. Make sure you build in review sessions and plenty of practice. If you have a y find she is only too willing to provide some in between sessions.

nd someone talking technospeak (see quote k them to explain what they mean and show e talking about. We all started somewhere and the simple actions and take them for granted, se the spell checker and create folders.

nospeak example

nd forward a jpeg of the new building to the press need a copy of your active database of customer essed in a zip file. Thanks.

performance

problems for even the most technically able is vith the pace of technological change. This was ng ago as 1998 by Stan Davis and Christopher

change accelerated way beyond your comfort zone? e just like everyone else . . . You're not imagining

Davis and Meyer (1998)

own in the rate of technology spending in city has not really slowed down. Indeed, it might be that the need for software producers to drive up earnings is why we are continually being bombarded with new versions of software and new devices.

You only need to be inactive for a few months to find that the software interface has changed and your IT skills have atrophied. Never mind changing your password, where has that icon that you customized gone? The problems are not quite so acute in small organizations or for those who work on their own, as you are more in control of when you upgrade (or even change) the software. Nonetheless, the question still remains as to how can you sustain your level of IT fitness and stay abreast of new developments and innovations, which might benefit you. Not surprisingly it's really all about immersing yourself in what is happening within the world of information and communication technology and/or having a friend or colleague who will guide you and help keep you up to date.

5.7.1 Immerse yourself in the technologist's world

Sir John Harvey Jones (when he was chairman of ICI) used to make a point of meeting his IT director every month for a discussion about current and emerging developments. These sessions were sacrosanct. This was in the early 1980s when the speed of technological change was far slower. The point being that he foresaw that even then, as chairman, he needed to be well briefed about technology and how it might impact the business. This is a belief he still holds:

> *Top managers hate appearing to be idiots. Pride often means that they will not ask anyone to do something that they could not do. But today the sign of a good leader is someone who will ask and that includes asking about IT. You should really think around how you could run your business with limitless computing power. To do that you need access to someone who understands what IT can do . . . Those who understand technology often don't understand business and vice versa.*
>
> Sir John Harvey Jones, April 2000, in an interview with Dr Seeley (part of which was published in *Director*, June 2000)

Not all of you will be a chairman and have quite the same priorities, but to keep pace with innovations and developments in IT means you must be prepared to walk the talk. Go and talk to those in the know and read some of the IT supplements which come with the daily newspapers and business magazines. Some of the more informative ones are listed in Table 5.1.

Table 5.1 Sources of technology briefings

Publication	Frequency	Source
Financial Times	Bimonthly	Web and print
Guardian	Weekly	Web and print
Telegraph	Weekly	Web and print
Times	Weekly	Web and print
Economist	Quarterly	Web and print
Business Week	ad hoc	Web and print
Director	Monthly	Web and print
Wall St Journal	Daily	Web and print
Silicon.com	Daily	Web

Have you ever thought of attending an IT trade show? Yes, they are loaded with technology but they are also a wonderful way to see what else is available. If you have an IT fitness coach maybe this could be one of your learning activities. It can help make the experience more meaningful to have a personal translator who can translate the technical sales babble into business benefits.

All too often managers complain that they do not understand technology. When asked when was the last time they went either to a technology briefing, or read a technology-focused article the response is usually in the negative. There is an argument which says if you buy a car you are not interested in learning about the engine. Nonetheless, you are prepared to enter a car showroom to pick your model. You cannot expect to keep in step with today's information communications technology and email devices if you don't enter into the technologist's world in some way or another as outlined here.

5.7.2 Keep a learning log

There will be functions and features, which you come across and use infrequently. Chances are you will then be frustrated that you cannot remember how to use them next time and slip back into old habits. One way to compensate for this is to keep a simple log of how you tackled the problem last time. The log can be either a dedicated notebook or just part of your daybook.

Make a permanent note of the menu where the function is located and how to use it. Maybe even print out the relevant help page and paste it into your learning log. (Of course if you are a paperless person you can do all this electronically in Word or a similar application.) The essential point is to keep a record of the function (or feature) you used, where to find (within which menu) and any key steps you performed to execute the task. A typical example is the 'out of office' auto reply. We could live off caviar if we were paid for every time we reminded a client how to use this feature.

You could also use your learning log to record tasks you think you could do more quickly but are not sure how to proceed. Then refer to it during a training session with either your IT fitness coach or mentor.

5.7.3 Have a booster session

From time to time have an IT fitness makeover with an IT fitness coach. Reassess your level of email IT fitness and make sure you are still comfortable with all the key functions.

5.8 Summary

This chapter has explored the techniques deployed by the committed users to maintain their optimum level of IT fitness and keep at the forefront of technological innovations. These tried and trusted keep fit exercises help them to ensure that they:

- maintain their profile as a good email citizen;
- continue to develop their level of email IT fitness as appropriate;
- do not suffer any dramatic skills loss;
- maintain their ability to control the ratio of noise to information in their inbox;
- spot new and emerging technologies that might benefit them.

This is a ten-point summary plan to help you develop and maintain you goal level of email IT fitness.

5.8.1 Ten tips to developing and maintaining IT fitness equilibrium

1. Identify your current level of email IT fitness and the gaps.
2. Determine what level of email IT fitness you want to achieve.
3. Check your current mental approach to using IT.
4. Make sure you have set yourself SMART goals.
5. Decide when and where you will do your learning.
6. Identify what would be the best learning approach for you.
7. Locate the necessary training materials (and people).
8. Block out time for your email IT fitness program.
9. Keep a learning log as a reminder especially for the infrequent but nonetheless crucial tasks.
10. Make sure you occasionally recalibrate your email IT fitness.

This ten-point plan should help you reap a real and ongoing return on your investment in your IT fitness plan. It should ensure that you keep within or even grow your optimum level of IT fitness be it bronze or gold.

6

Auditing your inbox

How do I know which emails I really want to receive?
How can I measure and reduce the level of noise in my inbox?
How can I stop all the unwanted emails?

6.1 Introduction

You have reviewed your personal management processes (Step 1 of the Mesmo model), boosted your personal level of email IT fitness (Step 2), and saved yourself about 20 to 45 minutes per day dealing with your email. Yet, you still feel you are spending too long dealing with your inbox. What next? This is where it gets tough – Step 3 auditing your inbox. However, this is where you can gain a quantum return at the personal level. It entails being ruthless about what information you really need to execute your job. We all love gossip but gossip on the email line can be time consuming in more ways than one.

Saying no is always hard. In today's world of e-communications saying yes may be almost as difficult. But doing nothing is now the most popular and time-wasting option in business email:

> *There are two words that are particularly useful when dealing with business requests. One is yes and the other is no. Both of these words are now in danger, particularly the second one. They have been supplanted by a third response: nothing. Every day at work we all receive dozens of questions by e-mail and voicemail that need a reply.*
>
> Kellaway (2002)

The questions are: How many of these did you really need to receive in the first place? How many do you need to action? How many are not really necessary, are just for background information and will remain untouched and eventually sink to the bottom of your inbox and into the recycle bin? How many were addressed directly to you? How many were cc'd? Those who have an inbox high in information, low in noise and which contain the fewest emails have all done an audit of one form or another:

> *It has taken us eighteen months to change the culture – it wasn't easy. I try to lead by creating the role model. For example, unless you tell people thanks but no thanks, they will keep copying you in. You've got to be blunt. I tell people – don't send me that again. Over the years I have become good at knowing what I want to see.*
>
> Bob, managing director of an international software house

This chapter provides you with a template to audit your inbox and in particular enables you to:

- identify the emails which are raising the level of noise;
- determine which emails you should banish from your inbox;
- reduce the number of unwanted emails which creep into your inbox;
- limit the damage caused by the less useful but still required emails.

Using the QSPER process described below should help to reduce further the time you spend on email.

6.2 The QSPER process

Auditing your inbox to identify what you really want to see is relatively easy, although it may take you a little time depending on the number you send and receive. The really hard part can be deciding what to eliminate. If you have a high noise, high information inbox the chances are that you are a hoarder and are loath to throw away anything, just in case you might need it.

The nub of the QSPER auditing process is to identify those emails which you really do not need and which add no value to how you perform. Indeed they may be losing you opportunities as they mask the ones you do need. Even if you leave them unopened there is still a cost to you, as there will come a point when you will need to delete them. There is also the time and cost of your time as they download into your inbox (regardless of whether you are working in an organization or on your own).

The QSPER inbox auditing methodology is a five-step sequence as shown in Figure 6.1 and outlined below.

Step i **Q**uantify the volume of traffic through your inbox.
Step ii **S**egment the content into those for action and those for information.
Step iii **P**rioritize the value of each email to you.
Step iv **E**liminate the unwanted email from entering your inbox in future.
Step v **R**eview noise to information levels and reaudit as required.

These steps are now described in more detail and some templates are provided to help you do your own QSPER audit.

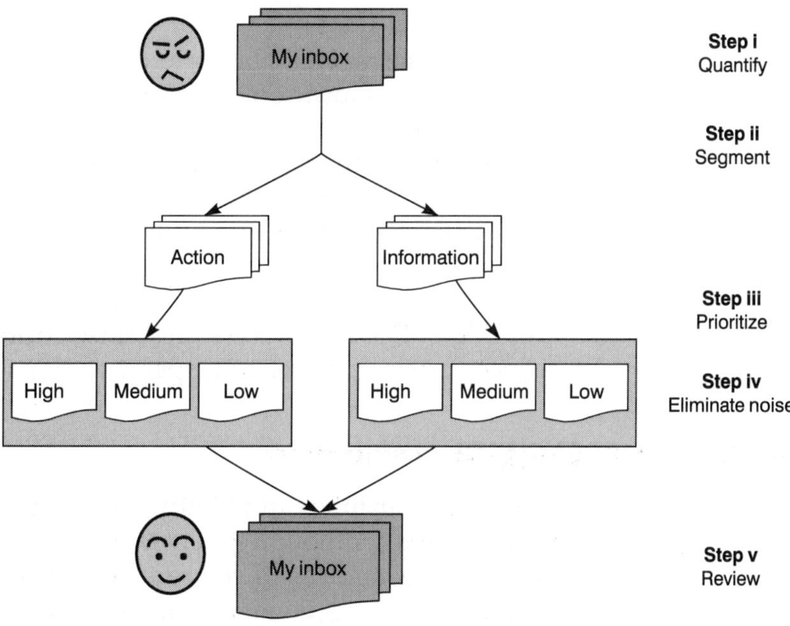

Figure 6.1
The QSPER inbox audit process

6.2.1 Step i – Quantify the volume of traffic

First, measure the actual volume of email you receive and send on a typical day. For most people this is mid-week as traffic tends to peak at the end of the week when everyone madly tries to tidy up their desk and shorten their 'to-do list' as shown in Figure 6.2.

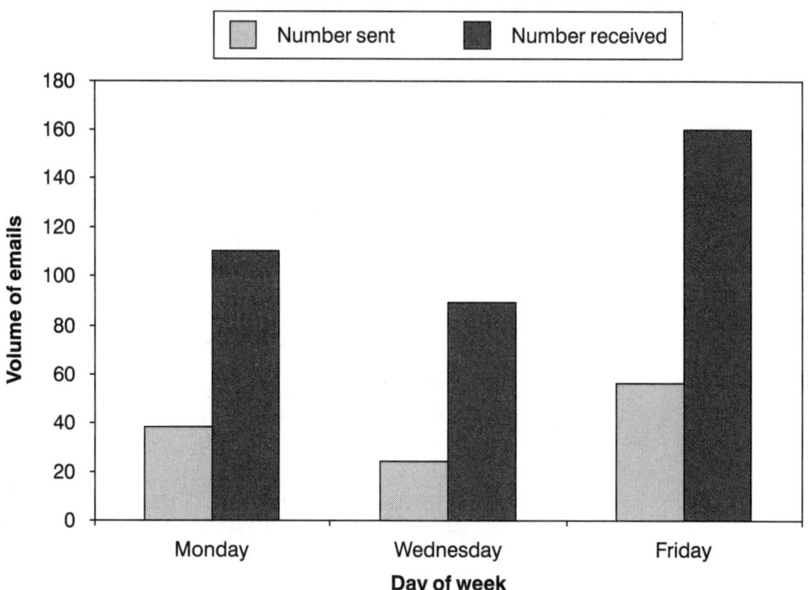

Figure 6.2 David's email traffic through the week

Similarly there is often a backlog on Monday from those who choose to work over the weekend. You might want to monitor the traffic through your inbox over a few days and even over specific times during the day to spot any unusual trends. Try completing the email traffic template in Table 6.1 for a typical week and for one day within the week, as volumes will fluctuate and tend to fall off near holiday periods, e.g. Bank Holidays, Christmas.

> **The contours of my inbox**
> How does your ratio of sent to received compare with the norm?
> What patterns emerge with your inbox?
> What do you think is the cause of any spikes?
> What action can you take personally to smooth the spikes?

Generally, the ratio of received to sent is 3:1. It does make you wonder who is doing all the sending. Your ratio of sent to received email will also tell you something about the noise level of your

Table 6.1 Measuring the weekly email traffic flow

Traffic through the week

Direction	Monday	Wednesday	Friday
Received			
Sent			
Ratio sent to received			

Typical daily flow of traffic

Time	Before 9.00	9.00 to 11.00	11.00 to 13.00	13.00 to 15.00	15.00 to 17.00	After 17.00	Total
Received							
Sent							

inbox, for example high noise/low information inboxes are often nearer 1:1, that is for every email you receive you instantly bat one back.

Look for any patterns and possible easy solutions to gain a quick win in terms of reducing the overall traffic as discussed in Chapters 1 and 2 based on your preferred executive lifestyle.

6.2.2 Step ii – Segment the content

Pick a typical day and now segment the incoming email according to whether it is for action or information: an example template is shown in Table 6.2. Alternatively you might opt for grouping them by address, which is direct to you or copied to you.

6.2.3 Step iii – Prioritize the value of each email

Whichever grouping you choose, next prioritize each item according to how valuable they are to you. Some typical scales are shown in Table 6.3. This should quickly show you the source of the noise, i.e. those which have no specific deadline attached

Table 6.2 Segmenting your inbox

Category	Number received	% total number received
Action		
Information		
Total		

Table 6.3 Prioritizing your inbox

Subject	Number for action				Number for information			
	1	2	3	4	1	2	3	4
Key clients								
New CRM software project								
Personnel matters								
Budgets								
Competition								
Diary								
Meeting papers								
New York office								
General internal news and gossip								
Personal								
Miscellaneous								

Urgency of action/reading the information
1 = immediate
2 = during the day
3 = over the next few days
4 = no specific time

to them and are often only information. You might either be on the cc list or they are an e-newsletter (e.g. from a supplier, conventional newspaper or internet news provider).

You may find it more helpful to convert the data into a percentage of the total number received for that day. If you are the type for whom a picture is worth a thousand words then use a spreadsheet for the audit, as you can quickly chart the results. The results of a typical QSPER audit are shown for David Jones, the operations director of a government agency, in Figure 6.2 and in Figures 6.3 and 6.4 in the case history at the end of this chapter.

Other ways in which you can segment and prioritize the content of your inbox include by sender or by address (cc'd or direct to you). Scales of importance might be high, medium, low, deleted on receipt.

Use of other media and attachments

At this point you should also review the appropriateness of email as the media to use for the message. For example, would it have been quicker and easier to convey the information by phone, if you operate some type of shared electronic filing space, bulletin boards (for Notes users) or intranet. You might also want to assess whether any attachments could have been placed on one of these rather than sent to everyone. A suggested template for this is shown in Table 6.4. Alternative ways of circulating attachments are discussed in Chapter 15.

Regardless of how you choose to segment and prioritize your inbox and how deep you go (e.g. looking at the use of alternative media) you are now at the point of no return. Either, you choose

Table 6.4 Appropriateness of email

	Number	**% total inbox**
Appropriate		
Phone would have been more effective		
Meeting would have been more effective		
Other media would be better, e.g. intranet		
For attachments, other media would be better, original paper copy CD-ROM		

to live with and accept the state of your inbox and attendant consequences, or you must decide how to embargo some if not all of the unwanted emails.

6.2.4 Step iv – Eliminate the unwanted email

To most people nothing is more troublesome than the effort of thinking.

James Bryce (1901) *Studies in History and Jurisprudence*

The emails which you regard as *non-essential* may be creeping into your inbox and causing a noise for a variety of reasons as indicated in Chapter 1, such as:

- people playing politics;
- a cover my backside culture;
- projects in which you are no longer interested;
- newsletters that have lost their appeal or relevance;
- you have changed roles but still receive emails relating to the old role.

The primary action to take is to return all this intrusive noisy email.

Return to sender with a polite explanation of why you no longer need it

Many find this hard to do; perhaps it is all part of our need to make everyone loved? Yet those who use email extensively but have the least noise are very good at simply asking 'Why have I been sent this email?' This is the question the managing director of an international services and logistics organization frequently put to his peers and subordinates with great effect. He now very rarely receives more than 20 emails a day, all of which are of high priority.

> **Five quick ways to remove the irrelevant emails**
> Return to sender with a polite explanation of why you no longer need it.
> Apply the email by exception rule.
> Unsubscribe to unwanted newsletters.
> Inform the IT department about junk mail you receive.
> Encourage the use of shared information areas.

Many managers receive 'position' emails – ones from people who believe they can help because they are the boss. This is how one manager deals with such requests:

> *I am often sent emails for action because of my grade. I send them back saying X is the person in the team who can really make that happen for you. Nine out of ten times it works and I don't need to get involved again.*
>
> Andrew, IT director of a government agency

Another source of intrusive email is when a person has changed jobs but others still believe that person is the one to deal with their request:

> *I just had three emails asking me what quantity of tickets we should order. You know, the tickets to label our bags of widgets. Now I am the general manager this is not my responsibility so I passed them on to Fred the new operations manager. But they still keep emailing me!*
>
> George, regional general manager, manufacturing company

In cases of changing responsibilities it is not enough to forward the email. You absolutely must tell the sender who is now responsible for the job. Otherwise mushroom management will persist and you have only yourself to blame if emails like this continue to invade your inbox.

Apply the email by exception rule

Try applying the email by exception rule. This is especially useful when subordinates and peers keep sending you progress notes on projects. Tell them you trust them and really only want to be told of exceptions and impending problems, rather than regular updates just to say everything is on schedule.

Unsubscribe to unwanted newsletters

If you are on an inappropriate circulation list ask to be removed. Similarly, take a long hard look at all those e-newsletters, etc. and ask yourself which ones have contained any really useful juicy killer information over the last month. Unsubscribe from those that do not add value. Many e-newsletters and e-direct mail will somewhere have a link to click on if you wish to 'unsubscribe'. If not just reply and put 'unsubscribe' in the subject line. This may take a couple of minutes to instigate but you will be well rewarded, as it will save you much more than two minutes over the coming weeks.

Companies are becoming much more protective of their brand and sensitive to being seen to spam. Therefore most organizations will comply with your request. If they don't a follow-up email with a more stern warning about the Data Protection Act usually works wonders.

A problem can arise if the original recipient has left and you have taken over their inbox. Again patience and persistence do work.

Inform the IT department about junk mail you receive

Most email management and anti-spam software works on the principle of knowing the name of the sender to block. Your IT department will have a list of the common and well-known names and source of junk mail, but new ones are always emerging. Maybe you have a persistent company in your specific market place from which you do not want to receive emails. If you do not tell your IT department how else will they know what else you want blocking at source?

The VP marketing of one of the leading email management software houses continually scans his inbox for junk mail to see what is new and what has been missed by their software. He recommends that 'you don't subscribe to too many newsletters' as this is a seeding ground for new spam and junk mail. His motto is 'bin the junk mail but not before you have forwarded a copy to the IT department.'

Encourage the use of shared information areas

All too few organizations exploit the power of shared information areas such as discussion zones on internal websites, bulletin boards (for Notes users) and personal portals. Complacency rules when it comes to sending one set of information (be it a one line email or a set of attachments). Everyone says they are fed up but few take action. The use of shared areas is discussed in more detail in Part Three – The corporate perspective.

6.2.5 Step v – Review the noise to information level and reaudit

Over time, you may find you need to reaudit your inbox. For example, your role may change and hence both your killer information needs and responsibilities will change. E-newsletters that were once very informative might become less useful. If the level of noise starts to creep up, be prepared to review your inbox.

6.3 Case history – David, Operations Director, government agency

When David took up his new post he was receiving an average of 100 emails a day. His office would prioritize and move them to subfolders within his inbox. The urgent ones were dealt with as quickly as possible. Jo, his principal PA, was spending nearly all day dealing with his inbox. She listed all the non-urgent ones and if David needed to see the full text he would ask her to run it off. David was spending every Saturday afternoon clearing the backlog of non-urgent emails, which built up during the week. Both he and his PA just felt bogged down by it all.

They knew something was wrong and far too many emails were flowing into his main inbox, but they could not see exactly what was causing the build-up. Was it too many cc'd emails, information about projects others thought David should be aware of, final copies of documents David had already commented on, etc. This is what an audit over a week revealed.

6.3.1 Spread per day

David was receiving about 20 new emails every two hours (roughly one every six minutes). Every time Jo went to make coffee the inbox looked like the stock market on a bad day – another tidal wave of red was making its way across the screen.

6.3.2 Ratio of action to information

As shown in Figure 6.3 this revealed that on average only 35 per cent required David to take action. The remaining 65 per cent were sent to him for information.

The questions now were which projects did all emails relate to? and how urgent was it that he read them (regardless of whether they were for action or information)?

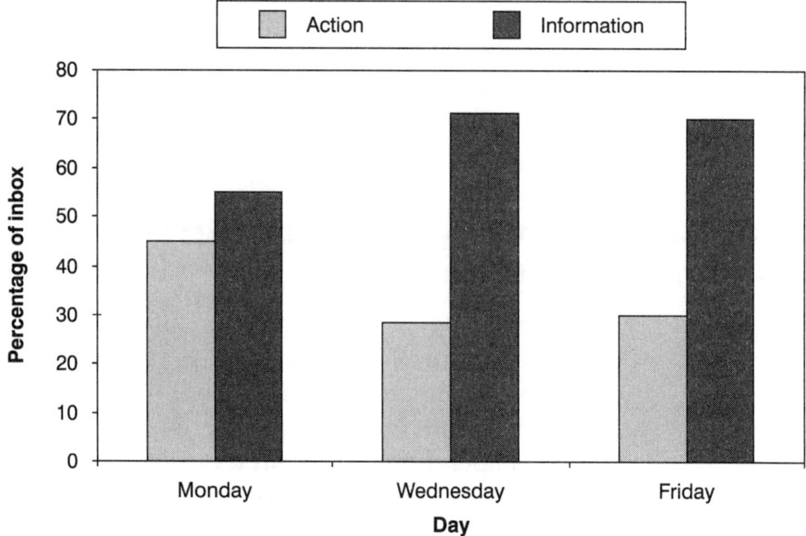

Figure 6.3
David's inbox – the ratio of action to information

6.3.3 Content and urgency

As shown in Figure 6.4, a detailed audit for the Wednesday through 'David's Inbox' highlighted that while some of the 'for information' emails did require David to read them, by the end of the week at least 35 per cent had no deadline attached to them.

The audit by content revealed that on average 15 per cent related to papers sent out by his division and about which he needed to be aware but which he did not read as he had already signed off

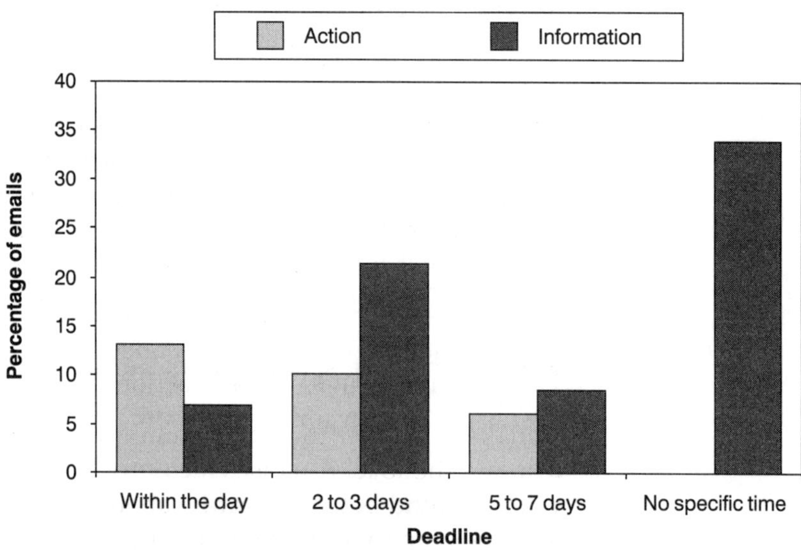

Figure 6.4
Deadlines for David to read his emails

the draft. Emails about meetings (either setting the date or papers for future ones) occupied about 17 per cent of the daily traffic. Taken together on a daily basis about 32 per cent of his inbox contained emails that he really did not need to see. Not surprisingly this was the dross that Jo filtered out and printed off, just in case David wanted to see them. Ninety-eight per cent of the time her judgement was correct and the paper file of such emails lay untouched.

The audit showed up in stark relief what everyone suspected, that too much noise was blocking up the main inbox.

6.3.4 The solution

The quick fix was to divert all the unwanted emails into subfolders, for example those relating to Project B and meetings. His team were asked to put an appropriate title in the subject line (e.g. Project B or meetings), which could then be picked up by the rule used to filter this type of email.

David then discussed the results of the audit with his team. It was clear that they copied him on email because he was the boss and this is how the division had always operated. He was seen as the hub for all discussions about ongoing projects.

David decided to change the culture and adopt the 'email by exception rule'. He was no longer to be copied in on every conversation his team had about projects in general. This represented quite a change in management style especially for an organization steeped in a culture of bureaucracy. He also encouraged them to talk to him more rather than send an email; this was welcomed by the team.

David is now also exploring the use of a shared area and a discussion zone on his personal website to improve the flow and management of the one-to-many type of emails (especially the conversational logs on which he was copied just because everyone felt he needed to know what was being discussed).

The five key benefits the audit has started to deliver are to:

- lessen the time spent by both himself and his office handling his inbox;
- make it quicker to spot the important emails;
- lower the level of noise;
- keep David better informed about key issues;
- reduce the total volume of email traffic across his division.

It was only once he had audited his inbox and personal information needs that he could start to change communications patterns and information flows to use email more effectively.

6.4 Summary

This chapter has shown you how you can audit your inbox to highlight and identify the real causes of the noise. Second, it has shown you some key steps to reduce unwanted email intruding into your inbox. As Mintzberg once said about creating strategy:

> *Real strategic change requires not merely re-arranging the established categories, but inventing new ones.*
>
> Mintzberg (1994)

The final leap to rebalance the ratio of noise to information in your inbox will require a similar reassessment of your use of email to communicate with people to satisfy your and their appetite for information. But if you are not prepared to confront change then you may need to learn to live with a busy inbox and lost opportunities.

7 Managing stress in the email office

Have emails added to your workload?
Does your email inbox sometimes feel overwhelming?
Do you ever feel out of control in the email office?

7.1 Introduction

Wherever we are today, the email office is never far away. At home, at work, in the hotel or the high street or even while travelling, it is ever present. The sight of someone with a laptop tapping away furiously on a train or on a plane is now a sight many of us take for granted. Mobile phones and the opportunity to download and read emails seem to be everywhere. In addition voicemail ensures we cannot miss any calls even if we have more than enough to do and would be glad not to have to return them. There seems to be no hiding place from the email office!

7.2 How the email office causes stress

For all the advantages that these breakthroughs in technology bring, there are of course 'downsides', and additional stress can be one of them. Emails have become another pressure on already hectic workloads. Emails may add to an individual's stress for the following reasons:

- They don't really know how to use their computer or particular software packages.
- 24 hour communication and the extended day.
- The sheer volume of daily emails adding to a busy workload.
- Being more contactable – at home, on holiday, during business trips.
- Emails awaiting your return from time out of the office.
- A greater sense of urgency and shorter deadlines.
- Fear of viruses.
- Eye strain.
- Muscle tension – caused perhaps by inappropriate equipment, e.g. unsuitable chair, incorrect desk height, etc.
- Unnecessary or junk emails wasting your time.
- Receiving abrupt and upsetting messages sent by someone equally or even more stressed!
- Staying on in the office too long or working too late at home to clear the backlog of emails.

When managers are asked what are the main workplace stressors, the increase in technology in general, and more specifically emails, always appears in the top ten. For many the sheer volume of emails places an enormous demand on the working day. If not managed effectively, it can become a major contributor to workplace stress.

The demands of mobile phones and voicemail can also add to the pressure. Has your phone ever rung at a highly inconvenient time, perhaps right in the middle of a conference, or as you are rushing to catch a train? Do other people's phones annoy you – not only the sound of the ringing but also the type of conversation many people have on them? The electronic office can be a stressful place.

7.3 What is stress?

Stress is a normal part of everyday life. Managed effectively it can work in a positive way to enrich our lives and help us to perform more effectively. Badly managed, or not managed at all, stress can be a killer.

Stress is the response by the body (mental and physical) to the demands and pressures placed on it. The amount of pressure will determine whether we can cope or not:

- Enough pressure for our coping abilities and we can live a healthy and happy life.
- Too much pressure for our coping abilities and we may suffer stress related illnesses.
- Too little pressure may also result in suffering from stress – the stress of boredom, worthlessness and lack of self-esteem.

Stress management is therefore an issue of, on the one hand, managing the demands and pressures placed on us and, on the other, our coping strategies.

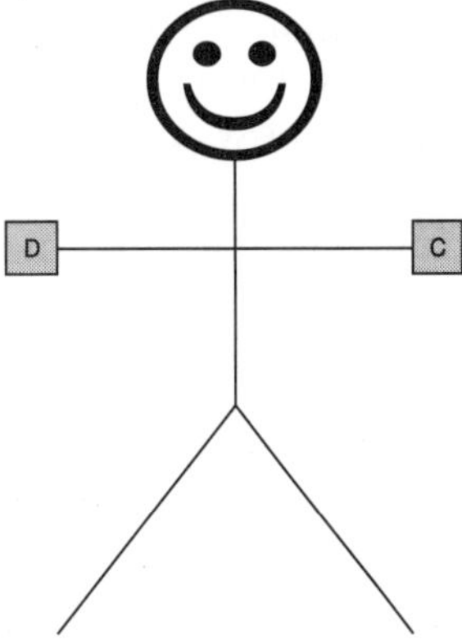

Figure 7.1
Demands are balanced to coping strategies

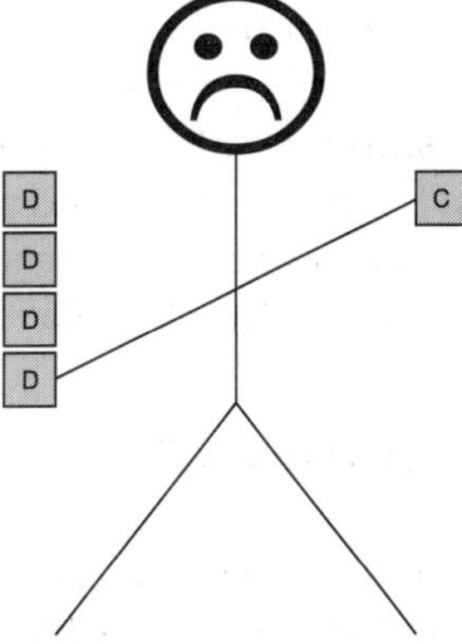

Figure 7.2
The unbalanced demands and coping strategy

The point where positive pressure turns to negative stress will be different for each individual. It will also be different at various times in our lives. This presents another challenge when we try to manage stress in our lives and the lives of those around us. For many the pressures of the email office can be the additional demand that turns positive pressure of an enjoyable job and balanced working life into negative stress. How often has an email first thing in the morning or last thing at night been the straw that broke the camel's back.

7.4 Symptoms of stress – the downward slope

7.4.1 Some early warning signs

The following are lists of common physical, mental and behavioural symptoms of stress. As personal stress increases more of these symptoms are likely to become apparent. By noticing how many of these items you are currently experiencing, either continuously or from time to time, you can obtain an early warning of an increase in stress. Even though some of the symptoms may have a clear physical cause, count them nevertheless, for their occurrence is still likely to be an indirect consequence of stress.

Emotional signs

- irritability
- more suspicious
- more gloomy, depressed
- more fussy
- feeling tense
- drained, no enthusiasm
- under attack
- cynical, inappropriate humour
- alienated
- feeling nervous, apprehensive, anxious
- feeling of pointlessness
- loss of confidence
- less satisfaction in life
- demotivated
- reduced self-esteem

Physical signs

- headaches
- indigestion and stomach ache
- palpitations – throbbing heart
- breathlessness
- nausea – feeling sick
- muscle twitches
- tiredness
- vague aches or pains
- skin irritation or rashes
- susceptibility to allergies
- excessive sweating
- clenched fists or jaw
- fainting
- frequent colds, flu or other infections
- recurrence of previous illnesses

Mental signs

- indecision
- memory failing
- loss of concentration, easily distracted
- tunnel vision
- bad dreams or nightmares
- worrying
- muddled thinking
- making mistakes
- less intuitive
- less sensitive
- persistent negative thoughts
- impaired judgement
- more short-term thinking
- hasty decisions

Behavioural signs

- unsociability
- restlessness
- loss of appetite or overeating
- loss of interest in sex, or overuse
- disturbed sleep or insomnia
- drinking more alcohol
- smoking more
- taking work home more
- too busy to relax
- not looking after oneself
- lying
- anti-social behaviour
- unable to unwind
- low productivity
- accident prone
- bad driving
- impaired speech
- voice tremor
- increased problems at home
- poor time management
- withdrawing from supporting relationships

Below are some indications of stress (based on Hargreaves (1998)). To establish your general level of stress answer the questions below as honestly as you can. Use the following scale:

1 = Never
2 = Seldom
3 = Sometimes
4 = Frequently
5 = Nearly all the time

		Score
1	I tire quickly	
2	I am more nervous than others	
3	I have regular headaches	
4	I work under a great deal of tension	
5	I worry over money and business	
6	I sweat very easily even on cool days	
7	I notice my heart pounding and shortage of breath	
8	I have stomach troubles	
9	I have had periods in which I have lost sleep over worry	
10	I frequently find myself worrying over something	
11	I wish I could be as happy as others seem to be	
12	I feel that difficulties are piling up so high that I cannot overcome them	
13	I have at times worried over something that really did not matter	
14	I feel useless at times	
15	I am inclined to take things hard	
	Total score	

7.4.2 What your score means

15–30 A low score means that you are a relaxed person and not likely to be suffering from stress

31–45 This range of score indicates a good level of control most of the time. Some situations cause stress occasionally. Look again at the questions you scored the highest

46–60 This range of score means you suffer from stress and are likely to be experiencing some stress related illnesses

61–75 This range indicates a high level of stress. You will most likely be suffering from some stress related illness

7.5 Summary

7.5.1 Anxiety

Remember you are in charge! If you are unsure how to use the internet, or are anxious about viruses, get one of the easy-to-understand manuals, go to a class or ask an understanding computer buff to explain what you need to know – at your pace.

7.5.2 Constant interruptions

It is not essential to have mobile phones on all the time. People will ring back if they are that keen to speak to you. To prevent your mobile ringing at an inappropriate time get into the habit of turning it off. To stop other people getting frustrated only use your phone when really necessary and keep your conversations brief. As for those voicemails – only answer the ones that are important. Those people who ring leaving useless or unnecessary messages will soon tire of doing so if silence is the response.

7.5.3 Muscle tension

Ensure, when you are using any type of computer, that you are able to sit correctly, with sufficient support, and that it is easy and comfortable to use the keyboard. Using incorrect workstations, balancing the laptop on your knees, using it stretched out on the floor, or on a bed is not recommended.

7.5.4 Eyestrain

Many of us spend far too long looking at computer screens. It is no wonder our eyes feel the strain. Make sure you take regular breaks and do eye exercises from time to time. First, look at something close at hand and then change your focus by looking at something as far away as possible.

7.5.5 Tiredness

The common cause for this can be those very late nights sitting in front of that screen sending messages or trying to read a mountain of messages that have been sent to you.

7.5.6 Irritability and frustration

You may experience these as a result of receiving abrupt and upsetting messages. Do you feel like retaliating? Does the volume of emails, mobile calls and voicemail messages you receive frustrate you? Never forget there is only so much you can do. Retaliating does not usually help – if anything it can add to your problems. We feel irritated and frustrated when we perceive there are just too many demands on us or when we are upset by other people's actions. Being assertive and managing your time well can really help.

Part Two You and your team in the email office

For many people email has become the most commonly used form of written communication in the office. Most office-based people now send more emails per day than letters, memos or faxes. Email has become a main way of communicating among team members, between supervisor and employee and between company and customer. For many, particularly young people, it is also true for personal correspondence between friends and family. Many people entering business today may never have written a formal or business letter. Their main form of correspondence may only ever have been electronic.

We now use email for all forms of written communication – from job applications to letters of resignation, from meeting agendas to minutes, from invitations to letters of thanks and from a quick 'yes' or 'no' response to a major report. We send electronic birthday, get well and Christmas cards and we even use emails for the infamous 'Dear John' letter.

Emails have not only changed the way we communicate but also the way that we relate to people. It is not difficult to spend the whole day in the office without having a meaningful face-to-face conversation, either business or social with a colleague. Emails can be quickly typed and sent with the press of a button – hopefully the correct button. There are increasingly more cases of emails containing the most intimate details of an exciting weekend being sent out to the entire company database because the wrong button has been pressed! A well-crafted email can have the same positive impact as any other form of written communication. Equally an email written in haste can easily offend or upset the recipient, lose a reputation or client.

Emails know no boundaries and have therefore had a profound impact on the way people work within teams. The traditional manager/PA relationship has changed with many managers now being the direct recipient of emails rather than going via the PA. This has had an impact on what the boss sees first hand. The friendly advice from the PA to the member of staff about how to reword a letter or memo is, for many, a thing of the past. It also has an impact on the amount of information people receive and have to read and respond to. The morning ritual of going through the post with the PA is for many a thing of the past. The number of PAs in Britain has dropped by 35 per cent since the beginning of the 1990s. The spread of voicemail in the early 1990s, followed by email and handheld computers, has forced many managers to fend for themselves. With most managers now computer literate and able to type, many organizations are scrapping their typing pool. A further sharp fall in secretaries and PAs is expected when voice-operated software becomes more reliable and widely used:

> *Your secretary used to be responsible for managing your typographical errors. Now you have to master spell-check. She used to be able to screen your calls. Now outsiders get access to you through email. When you were on the road, maybe you called her once a day to get your messages. Now you spend time on the road dialling up your laptop.*
>
> Mark, senior executive of a global bank

Email has tied us to the office computer for longer working days but has also freed us up to be more flexible in our working patterns. It has meant that we do not need to attend so many meetings yet has made it easier to stay in contact with the office when away on business trips or on holiday.

The first part of this book looked at how you can gain control of the email office and make it work for you. This part looks at gaining maximum benefit from email in relation to working with other people and the impact that your emails have on them. It will look at:

- how to work effectively with your PA and establish a working relationship that will benefit you both;
- the best way to communicate using email, both in terms of content and layout;

- managing email on the move. What equipment do you need and what do you need it to do?
- the best ways to access your emails on the move. Business travel will never be the same again!

The following chapters contain various exercises that will help you assess how you can gain maximum benefit from the way you use email and work efficiently with the key members of your team. By following the guidelines you will be able to ensure that you are using the most appropriate equipment and getting the best from it.

8 Two people, one inbox: working with your PA

Is it still best use of my time for me to handle my own inbox?
How can my PA and I avoid dealing with the same e-mail twice?
How can I ensure my PA sees all my emails even if I deal with them?

8.1 Introduction

In the old days, pre-email, few managers would have dreamt of directly opening their own mail. It would wait in the in-tray until their secretary had date stamped and sorted it into the urgent, not so urgent and nice to know. In some cases the sender's missive might never even reach the intended recipient. The PA was seen as the gatekeeper in more ways than one. Your phone and correspondence would be diverted and filtered through your PA, and in some cases she even patrolled the physical access to your office.

But of course email has the potential to change all that, at least for those who handle their own email. After all, who can resist the temptation of opening an email sent direct to you with a subject line about something you are either interested in or responsible for? Maybe it's just to moan that the canteen food is awful. Or, it could be an interesting crumb of information about the competition. Of course you don't have to open the next one if you decide the sender is not saying anything of value.

Dealing with one's own email is to some extent a double-edged sword. On the one hand it opens this rich network of communications paths, which cut right across all conventional organizational boundaries. Email encourages people at all levels to communicate with others who they wouldn't normally contact directly. Many CEOs and MDs have told us that by this means they receive interesting and often very valuable snippets of information which they might not otherwise have heard until it was too late to take action. Andy Grove (1996) calls these senders his 'Cassandras of his business world'. They are people working at the coalface of the business who spot something that they feel Grove needs to know, for example who was signed into the visitors' book ahead of them.

On the other hand, handling your own email can be time consuming and create an ever-open door syndrome as this executive commented:

> *It enables you to get something in front of someone's nose, even if they don't want it. That's why my secretary filters my email. Otherwise people think I can always email him if I can't get past the secretary.*
>
> James, director of operations, insurance company

For many the dilemma is should they handle their own email or do they let their PA primarily deal with it, as they would have conventional mail? If they handle their own email then what is the impact on the role of the PA?

In this chapter we review:

- the boss–PA relationship;
- effective ways to work with your PA;
- how to store old emails when you both access the inbox;
- pros and cons of handling all your own email;
- the changing role of the PA.

8.2 Three options for working with your PA

There are three main ways of involving your PA in the process of handling your email as shown in Figure 8.1:

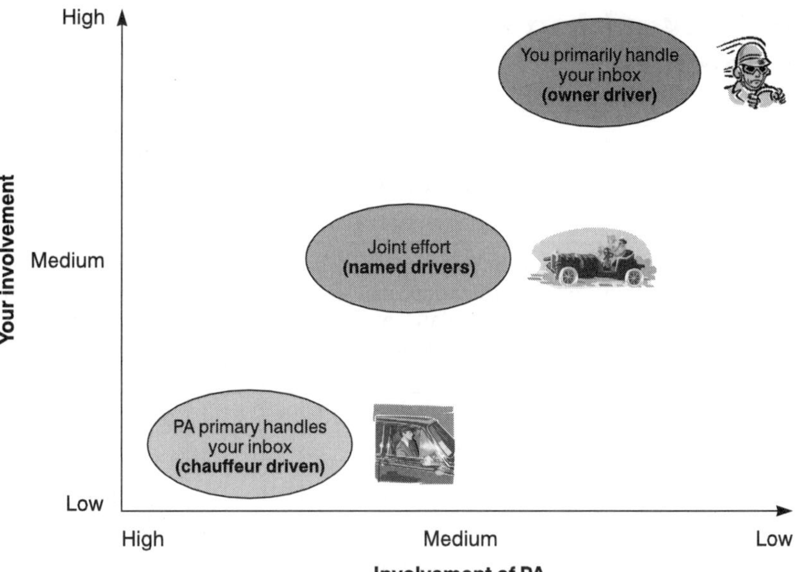

Figure 8.1
Who's driving the inbox

- 'Chauffeured' approach – your PA primarily handles your email.
- 'Named driver' approach – it is a joint effort.
- 'Owner driver' – you primarily handle all your email.

Of those who enjoy the bonus of having a PA handle their inbox is fairly evenly split across the three processes.

Whichever approach you take carries health warnings and before examining how best to make each way work there are two important caveats. First, there really are no absolute rights and wrongs – you must choose the way with which you are most comfortable and which adds the most value to your 'executive lifestyle'. Some of the leading captains of industry handle all their own email, while others adopt a chauffeured approach. Second, if you do involve your PA, no matter how extensively, the ultimate success will depend on the quality of your underlying working relationship with each other. Third, make sure you always keep your PA in the loop.

Before moving on to how to work the inbox together here is a short exercise to help you review your existing relationship with your PA and see if there is any need to make improvements.

8.3 Working with your PA: self-assessment exercise

This exercise highlights whether you are using your PA effectively. It is fairly searching, but often stimulates major potential for improvement.

1	I am more than happy that my PA knows about our organization, its latest developments and plans, and who are the major competition.	1	2	3	4	5	I'm not so sure that my PA knows much about our organization, its latest developments and plans, and who are the major competition.
2	I'm sure my PA knows what my job is, what I am trying to achieve, my major activities and deadlines.	1	2	3	4	5	I think my PA is only vaguely aware of my job, of what I am trying to achieve, why, and by when.
3	My PA knows what work is important for me, and knows how to protect my time.	1	2	3	4	5	My PA does not always know what work is important for me. He/she could improve our daily control by protecting my time.
4	I always sit down with my PA early in the day to communicate and plan.	1	2	3	4	5	I very rarely sit down to communicate and plan with my PA – especially early in the day.
5	After training, I can now delegate more important work to my PA, who already deals effectively with my low priority work.	1	2	3	4	5	There is much more routine work that my PA could handle, but we've yet to define how – and I have yet to train him/her to take on more important tasks.
6	We have developed a highly effective way of running our office and our workflow.	1	2	3	4	5	We could improve the way we organize our office and our desks.
7	We get on well together. We appreciate the best in each other, and are tolerant about our shortcomings.	1	2	3	4	5	Our personal relationship could be better.
8	I always let my PA know how he/she is doing, and I take time to train and develop his/her knowledge.	1	2	3	4	5	I've never really thought about appraising or training my PA.
9	My PA feels comfortable enough to point out my 'areas for improvement', and I do my best to achieve them.	1	2	3	4	5	The last thing I want to know from my PA is how he/she thinks I can do things better.
10	My PA is a great help in preparing for and following up my meetings.	1	2	3	4	5	There's a lot more my PA could do to help me prepare for and follow up my meetings.

8.4 Overall assessment

10		20		30		40	50

8.4.1 Interpretation

10–14 Excellent working relationship – a team
15–24 Very good utilization
25–35 Working relationship developing
36–45 Being used as a typist
46–50 Substantial PA underutilization occurring

8.4.2 Best practice

Your PA is one of the most valuable and immediate resources you have. They are also often the one you use least effectively.

PAs represent an area of huge potential that is seldom realized, which is not too surprising. Most PAs have been trained for their job and will have some, if not many, skills. However, *very few* managers are trained how to use a PA. Here are some guidelines that may help develop the working relationship between you and your PA.

Brief your PA on your business

Take time to brief your PA regularly on anything that will make them feel part of a successful organization – rather than just a tiny cog in a huge machine. Their induction course might well have been a long time ago.

Involve your PA in your diary planning

Brief your PA on your diary commitments and when you want to keep time free for yourself. A good PA is a tremendous help in guarding your diary from becoming overcommitted. It is also very much to their benefit – you will be turning important work around earlier.

Delegate higher priority work

It enriches their job, gives them greater job satisfaction, and relieves the pressure on you.

Beware of 'bad manners'

We can all be guilty of these occasionally – failing to let your PA know your whereabouts, failing to return telephone calls that they screened for you, leaving them to 'cover' for you, etc.

Thank you

It costs little to say it, but it goes a long way.

8.5 How effectively are you and your PA managing your inbox?

Read the following statements and tick the box which most closely corresponds to your opinion of how you and your PA work together to manage your inbox. Score 3 for Yes, 2 for Sometimes and 1 for No and then add up your score.

Statement	Yes	Sometimes	No
The way my PA prioritizes my inbox is a very accurate reflection of my needs			
I always make sure my PA is kept in the picture			
We work within a clearly defined process for handling email			
We review regularly the processes we use to handle my inbox			
We are always trying to improve the protocols we use to manage the inbox			
Emails are only ever handled once by one of us (i.e. you don't both open and reply to the same email)			

My score ____

Interpretation of your score

18 to 15 points You are working well together

14 to 10 points There is probably some wasted time and effort and hence scope for improvement
9 to 6 points You are probably not handling the inbox very effectively and efficiently as a team and should consider how you can save each other time (and maybe some stress)

Here are some ways you can improve how you work the inbox together, according to which approach you decide to adopt: chauffeured, named drivers, or owner driver.

8.6 The chauffered approach

8.6.1 Case history – Alex and Sandra

Alex is the finance director of a medium-sized UK retail company. He has been in his current post for about seven years and Sandra, his PA, has worked with him all that time. Alex spends much of his time in meetings both on and off site. He has a silver level of IT fitness, but by and large Sandra deals with his email. He only deals directly with his inbox outside normal office hours. He receives about 40 emails per day. Here is how they work.

Sandra works directly from within Alex's inbox and her own. She reads all Alex's emails and deals with those where she knows what's required, e.g. agreeing a meeting. Alex has a very clear organization chart, which describes exactly who is responsible for which tasks, e.g. bought ledger, treasury function, and bad debt collection. Sandra will forward any emails, which relate to one of these functions to the relevant person.

Where there is a follow-up action she creates a reminder in her calendar. Emails, which are directly for Alex, are then sorted into four folders:

'Very urgent' – must deal with today
'Urgent' – need to be dealt with over next two days
'Medium priority' – need to be aware of this
'FYI' – (for your information)

When Alex is in the office he will look in the folders and deal with the contents and then move the email to one of three folders:

Actioned
Sandra to Action
Print

When he deals with an email himself and there is an action to follow up he copies in Sandra so she can keep track of it. On very busy days Sandra will print out the emails and place them in paper files marked up in the same way.

Alex uses the same process when he deals with his inbox when Sandra is not available: he moves emails to one of the above folders. Sandra then checks these and files the emails in the appropriate folder when she has finished with them.

When he sends a new email about which Sandra needs to be aware he will again copy her in. His staff know that when replying they must only use the 'Reply' button and not 'Reply All', otherwise he and Sandra end up with two copies.

Sandra and Alex have spent quite some time refining how they handle Alex's inbox and telling the department how they work and what Alex likes to see and how.

This process works well for them and Sandra is always kept in the loop. When someone contacts Sandra she will nearly always either know about or be able to locate the email to which the person is referring regardless of whether she or Alex sent it.

Some managers prefer their PA to sort their email by project rather than priority. Whatever set of names you use, the key is to make sure you both agree on what goes where. This can sometimes take time to refine, so be prepared to review the sorting process several times. The more you refine it the quicker it will be for you both and the more you minimize the chance of an important email going unread.

8.7 Named drivers

In this situation there is more direct active interaction by the boss, for example between meetings, while in transit using remote access, or from another office, etc.

8.7.1 Case history – Rosemary and Janet

Rosemary is the HR manager for a large public sector organization. She has been in this post for just under a year. Janet was PA to the previous HR manager. Both have worked in the organization for over ten years but this is the first time they have worked together. Rosemary deals with her own email whenever she is in her office and not either in a meeting or writing a report. She often sends emails before and after Janet leaves, and from home (as she works from home one day a week). Janet deals with the inbox when Rosemary is either out or in meetings.

Initially, they found they were often both handling the same email and Janet had great difficulty keeping track of what Rosemary had and had not actioned and sent.

Now, they have a similar process for managing the email as Alex and Sandra. When Janet is dealing with the inbox she will read and sort the email by project (Rosemary prefers this) except for very urgent ones, which are printed off. Rosemary can then either dictate or send a reply, depending on the available time.

Incoming mail which Rosemary deals with is again moved into a folder by Rosemary after she has read it (like those folders which Alex and Sandy use). For those which Janet needs to action, Rosemary will usually 'edit' the incoming email with her suggestions. She tries to take the time to use another colour for her comments as this makes it so much easier for Janet. Although it takes Rosemary an extra few seconds, it means Janet can use her time more effectively and again limits the scope for disasters and misunderstandings.

As they had not worked together before and Rosemary was new to the post it took them about three iterations to find the right pattern of labels for the folders for incoming email. They chose a set labelled by key project names and one called 'the boss'. An 'order of urgency', as Sandra and Alex used, did not work because on any given day the actual priority might be the project, even though the email might seem urgent as a response was needed quickly.

They also have a 'delete' folder into which Rosemary will move items for deletion. However, she leaves Janet to action the deleting process, as they tend to keep even deletable items for a week, just in case they are needed.

Again, Janet will often print off emails if Rosemary is exceptionally busy with wall-to-wall meetings or about to travel. Rosemary does not carry a laptop as most of her travel is within the UK and between offices. She can either dictate a reply in transit or log-in on arrival and send her own reply.

However, she is just experimenting with a palmtop, which Janet can synchronize and give her as she leaves the office. This way she can read the emails en route and deal with them immediately. The only downside of this approach is the size of the screen when the email is long and handling attachments is still tricky.

When Rosemary sends an email about which Janet needs to be aware, like Alex she copies it to Janet. Sometimes when Rosemary is very busy she will just scan her inbox quickly but not actually deal with it. On these occasions she resets any she has opened back to 'unread'. That way Janet will see them as new emails and deal with them accordingly.

They both use the calendar to help keep track of emails, which require action from either one of them or someone else.

When the office is really busy Janet will print a list of incoming emails for that day and together they will check the listing just to make sure nothing has slipped through the cracks. (This happened to Rosemary once when an email from a Minister was somehow overlooked.)

Again this process of moving mail once one party has dealt with it to an appropriate folder ensures that by and large an email is only handled once and nothing vital is lost. Rosemary and Janet worked hard at finding just the right names for the folders, and Rosemary was careful to feed back to Janet when emails were wrongly sorted. Janet too would chip in if she couldn't find an email Rosemary had sent or handled.

8.8 Owner drivers

You are master of your own inbox. Owner drivers of the inbox can range from managers in large international organizations who receive up to 150 emails a day to managing directors of their own companies who receive about 30 emails a day.

Typically, you will be a gold user and suffering some degree of email addiction. You might even have a high noise/high information inbox. The thought of someone else dealing with your email is beyond your wildest imagination. You probably stay connected even when on holiday through some means or another (and most usually through to a handheld device).

8.8.1 Case history – Barry

Barry is the European operations director for an international technology company. He often receives upwards of 70 emails a day. He deals with all his own email except those relating to diary matters. Pat, his PA, deals with his diary. Barry immediately forwards all such emails to her and copies in the sender.

He takes a handheld device wherever he goes and is known for the speed with which he will reply to an email (never more than three hours). This is how he has always worked and is quite happy to continue in this vein.

It does present a problem sometimes, as Pat cannot always deal with queries which relate to email conversations where Barry has not copied her in on the original. Nonetheless they survive, and Barry feels he is just as efficient, if not more so, than colleagues who delegate.

It must be stressed at this juncture that not all owner drivers 'rev' their inbox in the fast lane. Many take a calmer and less

Table 8.1 Different ways of driving the inbox

Criteria	Approach – advantages and disadvantages		
	Chauffeured	**Named drivers**	**Owner driver**
Managing the level of noise	Maybe hard as you may not know how much noise you really receive.	Easier as you will see the level of noise.	You are in total control and can quickly see the noise level increasing.
Required level of email IT fitness	Bronze is minimum.	Silver is minimum.	Silver to gold.
Good email citizenship	Actions always speak louder than words so may be harder to establish best practice.	Best placed to establish best practice and set the role model for both your own team and the organization.	Well placed to establish the role model, but email addicts needs to be careful in case everyone thinks they must be like you.
Use of your and your PA's time	If you are busy this may be a good use of your time, but your PA may get fed up of acting as the email postman.	Striking a balance means you both use your time well providing there is no duplication of effort.	Make sure you are not spending too much time on email. Make sure your PA does not feel excluded and a loss of power as the gatekeeper.
Developing a network of Cassandras	May be hard, as people know you don't read your own emails and are not sure if you see them all.	Easy as people know that by and large their email will reach your eyes.	Other email-centric Cassandras will welcome you with open arms into their network. Just make sure you don't increase the noise level so that it obscures the real information.

frenetic limousine approach. They effectively drive their inbox in the middle lane and stay off-line when on leave. They leave their PAs to sift and deal with the urgent emails when they are either on leave or out for more than half a day.

As we said at the beginning no one approach is definitively right or wrong, better or worse. It is about what works for you. Table 8.1 gives a summary of the pros and cons of each of these options for driving your inbox.

8.9 Two people, one set of archives

One of the main problems about working with either your PA or even another member of your team is storing and accessing the old emails.

8.9.1 Your inbox is over the limit

How many times have you had an email message like this one from your IT department.

You have exceeded you storage limit, please clear your inbox.

Ah, but you are busy, and anyway doesn't the IT department realize there is more to life than worrying about overcrowded inboxes? So, you ask your PA to 'tell the IT department to increase the limit'. A few days later the same messages comes back. Worse still you cannot send an email because you are so over the limit!

Server storage space costs money. Consequently, most IT departments are constantly berating their users to clear their inboxes as they have exceeded the limit. Indeed you are probably one of the first to wonder why on earth the IT department are asking for a new server.

It is not enough simply to file your emails in folders; these still take up space and count towards your personal allocation of space on the server. What you have to do is either:

- move the emails (and indeed folders) to your 'personal' folders, which actually reside on the hard disk of you PC; or
- archive the old emails (either onto another area of your PC or another media, the most common of which is a CD-ROM).

Now here is the rub when it comes to working with your PA. In Microsoft Outlook, once you either move emails to personal folders or 'archive' them they no longer become shared. That is, your PA can no longer log-in from her PC and access any of the

Table 8.2 Storing old emails

Method	Pros and cons	When is it the best option?
Move them to your PA's personal folders	They can only be accessed from your PA's PC.	When you are chauffeured and your PA is the principal driver of your inbox.
Move them to your personal folders	Same as above but in reverse.	When you are an owner driver and you are the principal driver of your inbox.
Store them on a CD	You can both access them and providing you have the CD (e.g. you are not home and the CD is in the office).	Very good for storing really old emails to which you rarely need to refer.

emails, which are either in your personal folders or have been archived on your PC. Personal folders are what the name implies and reside on the PC of the person who owns the inbox, i.e. you.

There are ways around this as summarized in Table 8.2. Obviously, providing you both have access to each other's PCs, it does not matter on whose PC the old emails are stored or in what way (as personal folders or archives).

This is a book about the process of working with your inbox, so for more detail about the technical aspects of archiving (and the pros and cons of this as a technique) you should consult either one of the technical manuals listed in the Bibliography or your IT department. The main point to note here is that once you have moved emails from your inbox it is no longer quite so easy to have shared access.

8.10 Summary

This chapter has provided advice and guidelines on how best to work with your PA when dealing with email. Most of the guidelines can also be applied when working as part of a small team and you need to share and access the email tidal wave with another member of the team.

The protocol and procedure for granting permission to your PA to access your email will vary from organization to organization and this is a matter on which you will need to seek help and advice from your IT department. The essence of this chapter is the management processes and principles of how two people can effectively and efficiently manage one inbox. The key points are summarized below.

8.10.1 Ten ways to save time managing your emails with your PA

1. Decide who will deal with what and when and then agree on which approach to adopt.
2. Agree on a folder structure that is meaningful to you both.
3. Be prepared to review and rework both the folder names and how you work together.
4. Decide on whose PC it is best to store the old emails.
5. Make sure you keep to the agreed processes.
6. Always mark as unread any emails you have skimmed but not properly dealt with.
7. Ensure emails are only handled once by one person.
8. Respect each other's way of working and provide each other with feedback about how it is going.
9. Keep your PA in the loop regardless of how extensively you involve him/her in dealing with your emails.
10. Remember, deal, delete and delegate still rules.

9 Communicating in the email office

Do you sometimes use email inappropriately?
Do some people annoy you because of the way they use email?
Do you wish some people would just talk to you rather than always send emails?
Does your organization have an email policy?

Recent research issued by a major internet service provider reveals that most people under the age of 25 have never written a formal letter and are signing business emails 'love and kisses'.

9.1 Introduction

Many of us could not imagine business without email. For most of us, our jobs would be much more difficult, if not impossible. Email has made communication faster and more inclusive as more people can be involved in decision making. In addition, it can also be tangible proof and an auditable record – a 'paper-trail' for many aspects of business.

Like all good things, email is also subject to abuse and misuse. Desk rage is the new office epidemic and this can be sparked by the daily avalanche of emails. For many people too many inappropriate and badly written emails are the curse of the modern office. The result of this is that many organizations are now examining how they and their employees can gain maximum benefit from email and address the more negative aspects of this business revolution. As email replaces more formal methods of communicating several key issues need to be addressed as organizations develop a strategy for managing email traffic. These issues include:

- When is it not appropriate to communicate by email?
- What are the key elements that need to be included in an email policy?
- How to implement and enforce an email policy.
- Introducing guidelines for writing effective and appropriate emails.

9.2 When is it not appropriate to communicate by email?

Never for performance appraisal, I would never use e-mail for that. I think when talking to people about how they have done in their job it is really, really important to do it face to face.
Jean, business development manager, global IT consultancy

While the use of email has become the preferred method of communicating for so many aspects of business life there are certain issues for which it is not the most appropriate method. This may be because the subject matter is of a more personal or delicate nature and therefore more suited to a face-to-face discussion. It may also be that a quick phone call or chat rather than a series of emails going backwards and forwards could deal with the issues.

Matters to do with someone's personal relationship with the business are best done face to face. This may include conversations about salary, benefits, objectives or performance, whether good or bad. It might be appropriate to go back afterwards and confirm the discussion so you have a formal record in writing, especially if the news is not so good.

Similarly, when complex issues are being delegated these are better dealt with in a meeting, certainly in the initial stages. This will particularly be the case when you want people to do something that they probably don't want to do:

In our company a very common way of persuading or influencing people to do something is to call people to a meeting and make a presentation. You can then build your argument and see if everyone agrees. You can check that you are carrying people with you on the way.

Peter, project manager, IT software company

Email is also not the best form of communication when the issue relates to something of a delicate nature because it will be important to pick up reactions from the other person's body language and other non-verbal signals.

9.3 Case study

This case study looks at the appropriateness of email, video-conferencing and face-to-face communication when discussing delicate situations.

9.3.1 Paul, head of research – multinational company

I would never send an email where I needed to have a much better sense of what the other person was thinking or where there were sensitivities involved. People can make catastrophic social errors in email just through the syntax of the style they use. So where you need to have discussion or need to see the whites of someone's eyes there is no substitute for physical contact. In these situations virtual meetings [videoconferencing] doesn't work either. There is more to communication than simple sight and sound. Human beings actually get physical feedback. I do a lot of conference speaking. I did one yesterday and got up at 4 am to do a video presentation to our office in Sydney. It's not the same thing, you can see the audience but it's not the same as standing with the audience. You actually don't get the feedback, it's the same as using a telephone.

If you are physically with them they tell you at a subconscious level what they can hear, whereas without being physically there you don't get that. The same is true of conversations. You tend to get a dumbing-down of the trivializations of conversation. It becomes less emotionally rich than being in the same room as the other participants. You see it also in web-based discussion groups. Here you get very rapid entrainment, so the very first two or three people in the discussion set the norm for the group. Because you can't see the other people involved and aren't visibly part of the group, you don't know whether that is the norm or not and you go along with it.

The other day I was in a discussion group and I was getting angry with one person and there was no point in trying to carry on. But then a whole bunch of people came in and said why stop as we have been finding the discussion interesting. But my gut feeling was that it had gone on too long and no one else was taking part. It was just two of us passing stuff backwards and forwards, but actually the group was enjoying it. Now if that had been in a physical group you would have seen that but you don't see it like that in a virtual email discussion.

This is a summary of the type of messages for which email is and is not appropriate:

Nature of message	Email
Annual appraisal	No
Confirm appraisal action points	Yes
Performance feedback	No
Delegating complex task	No
Update company policy	Yes
Meeting agenda	Yes
Thank you letters	No
Delicate decision requiring buy-in	No
Knowledge sharing or fact finding	Yes
Arranging meetings	Yes
Networking to keep in touch	Yes

9.4 What are the key elements to be included in an email policy?

A clear email policy will help prevent time wasting, protect the security of your systems and data and minimize the risk of legal problems. An email policy should include guidelines on the following.

9.4.1 Permitted use of the company email system

This will indicate what employees can use the email system for. It may state that employees can only use the company email system for business purposes. In reality, this is unlikely to happen and most organizations recognize that employees will use the system for personal emails as well. In reality it is very difficult to stop employees receiving personal emails and allowing some personal use of email may improve employees' morale, and even efficiency.

However the policy may limit personal use. It might prohibit:

- Excessive personal use of email. For example, transmitting large attachments or joining busy mailing lists.
- Inappropriate or illegal content. Offensive jokes can be a particular problem area.
- Engaging in illegal activities. For example, using email to harass someone or deliberately sending a virus.
- Encrypting personal email and attachments.
- Running a personal business while at work.

It may be possible to give employees separate personal email addresses. Email can then be filtered into separate business and personal folders.

9.4.2 The content of emails

Many organizations have developed guidelines in their policy that cover the style and tone that should be used in company email. For most organizations this is usually somewhere between the informality of a telephone conversation and the formality of a letter:

- Adopt a similar style as your contacts. A formal style may appear laboured and tedious to people who are used to quick, friendly emails.
- Some sectors and some nationalities have their own standards. For example, a law firm might send more formal messages than a new media company.
- Short emails can appear brusque.
- Typing in capitals is the email equivalent of shouting, and can be considered rude.
- Use a more formal letter style for formal documents or when approaching someone for the first time.

Set up your software's signature feature to add letterhead details and any disclaimer to your messages automatically. (See Chapter 4 for tips and hints on how to make best use of your software to save time.)

Specify what content is prohibited in company emails. This should include:

- sexist, racist or otherwise offensive material;
- defamatory material;
- content that is protected by copyright;
- links to inappropriate material.

9.4.3 Good practice for sending emails

Employees should use their own, password-protected accounts to send emails and passwords should be strictly controlled. Encourage the use of email rather than phone calls for communications you wish to keep a record of.

Encourage employees to think whether email is automatically the best form for internal communications. It might be quicker to speak to someone on the telephone or to walk to their desk or office.

Establish standards for outgoing messages

Set out what typeface, type size and colour should be used.

Consider putting a limit on the size of any attachments. Many internet service providers place restrictions on attachment size (e.g. 5 Mb).

Have rules for handling confidential information

The email policy may ban certain types of information from being sent by email. For example, lists of customers and information about new products. It might specify that some information can only be sent using encrypted email.

9.4.4 Explain the potential contractual significance of emails to employees

An email can be as contractually binding as any other form of communication. You may choose not to use email for any contractually significant communications, and insist that all such documents are sent by letter. Consider including a disclaimer on emails. For example, an extremely simple disclaimer might state:

> This email is confidential, and is intended for the use of the named recipient only. If you have received this message in error, please inform us immediately, and then delete it. Unless it specifically states otherwise, this email does not form part of a contract.

9.4.5 Good practice when receiving email

A company email policy will set out who should read incoming emails

- Generally, employees should read only their own emails (using their own passwords to access the system).
- Establish how you will handle emails sent to a general address you might have (e.g. info@company.co.uk). Assign responsibility for dealing with such emails and set up your technology so that only the relevant people can read them.
- The policy should also cover how incoming emails are handled when employees are absent (e.g. on holiday). A simple option is to use an auto-responder to send a reply saying how long the employee will be absent, and giving an alternative contact.

The policy should set out your security procedures for dealing with viruses

This will particularly show the procedure employees should follow for dealing with attachments.

Some organizations set a response time

It might stipulate that all incoming emails should be replied to, or at least acknowledged, within 24 hours. If you have a permanent connection to the internet, and contacts who are used to using email, you may find that a faster response time is more appropriate. Software is now available that can help filter and prioritize emails. (See Chapter 4 for the personal aspects and Chapter 15 for corporate solutions.)

The policy should also explain how unwelcome emails should be dealt with

For example:

- Ask employees to tell friends not to send them inappropriate emails.

- Delete junk emails (spam). It is not usually a good idea to respond to spam, even just to ask to be taken off a mailing list. A response confirms that the email has been sent to a live address.

9.4.6 Monitoring email

There are legal restrictions on how you can monitor employees' use of email, although this remains a grey area. The policy should inform employees how you will monitor emails, and for what purposes. This should also include a clause on email monitoring in your employment contracts. If you fail to do so, you will need to get consent if you want to perform checks.

Tell employees how email traffic is monitored

If you use monitoring software to produce a log of sent and received emails, you should make employees aware of this.

Explain that you reserve the right to read individual emails

You may inspect individual emails for 'specific business purposes', including:

- Establishing the specific content of transactions and other important business communications.
- Making sure employees are complying both with the law and with your internal policies.
- Preventing abuse of your telecommunications system.
- Checking emails when employees are on leave.

If you wish to make interceptions for other purposes (e.g. marketing), you will need the consent of both the sender and the recipient.

9.5 Implementing the organization's email policy

9.5.1 Before implementing the policy consider taking expert advice

Although many aspects of your email policy will follow standard guidelines, it may be worth consulting a solicitor or other advisor.

9.5.2 Make the policy available to everyone

- Ask employees to sign a copy to confirm they have read it.
- Refer to the policy in your employment contracts.
- Make sure managers familiarize themselves with the contents of the policy.
- Provide a contact name for employees who have any questions.

9.5.3 Put in place any software that will help implement the policy

Ask IT experts about automated solutions that can help you reduce potential problems. This might include:

- Monitoring software to provide a record of email traffic.
- Filtering software to help employees prioritize emails.
- Using auto-responder software to reply to emails when employees are absent.
- Using virus-checking and other security software.

These are discussed in more detail in Chapter 15.

9.5.4 Provide any training that is needed

Employees may need training in effective use of email software.

It is one thing to have a policy but another thing to enforce it. A policy that sits in a drawer or on a notice board is useless. Having gone to the trouble of writing a policy, make sure that it is properly implemented as discussed in Chapter 16.

9.6 Writing a good email

Like other forms of written communication email says many things about the sender and the organization. Emails are seen as a quicker and more casual form of communication than letters or reports and the writer will often take short-cuts in both style and layout. This can result in the clarity of the message being diluted and the recipient, i.e. the reader, becoming confused, irritated or upset. Emails are like any other form of written communication in that they convey a message and can become part of a permanent record. It is important to take care when writing emails that they convey the correct message in terms of content and the impression it gives of you and your organization. Here are some general guidelines on both layout and style.

9.6.1 Layout

As with all forms of communication it is important to write the email from the reader's point of view, not the writer's. It is therefore important in the layout to make it easy for the reader to gain a quick understanding of what the email is saying. If somebody is receiving 50 plus emails a day they need to be able to gain an instant feeling of what each message is.

Most written communications reflect one of two layouts (see Figures 9.1 and 9.2).

Email should reflect the second style (Figure 9.2) with the headline being the subject heading. If it is a longer letter or report, the key messages should be contained in the main email and the full letter or report supplied as an attachment.

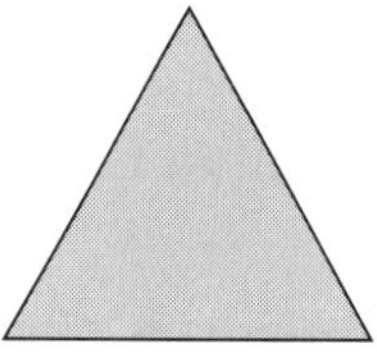

The basic triangle that gradually builds up the argument paragraph by paragraph. The final conclusions are contained at the end. This is the traditional report style and is also often used for more academic style articles.

This means that the reader has to read the complete report, gradually building up the arguments before they reach the conclusion. This is very thorough but can be time consuming.

Figure 9.1
Report style layout

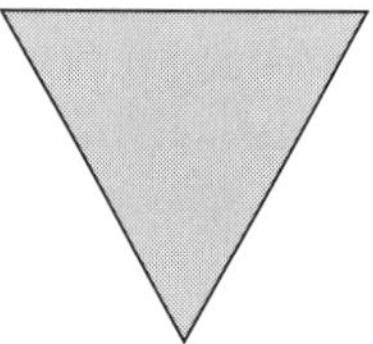

The inverted triangle layout hits the reader with the punchline first and then goes on to develop the message or argument. This is the layout used in newspaper articles that gives the message upfront in the headline and then goes on to develop it in the body of the article.

It is not uncommon with this type of layout to read the headline, first couple of paragraphs and then stop reading because they have all they need to know on the subject.

Figure 9.2
Headline layout

9.6.2 Guidelines on layout

Keep addressees to a minimum

Avoid the temptation to copy the world in on your email. People get annoyed at receiving unimportant or irrelevant emails. If you regularly copy people in on unimportant emails they are less likely to read the all-important one when you do send it. Remember that each email you send asks for someone's time.

Make the subject heading meaningful

Make sure it tells the recipient what the email is really about, e.g. 'Budget 2003' could mean a number of things, 'Allocation of Budget 2003' or 'Reduction in Budget 2003' makes it clear to the recipient what the email is about and may help to grab their attention.

Choose the appropriate greeting and use the person's name

For some people emails equal speed and thus short-cuts. Some people don't bother to start their emails with any greeting or finish with an appropriate sign-off. This can appear sloppy and rude especially in the business environment.

'Hi', 'Dear' and 'Hello' are the most common greetings and 'Kind regards' or 'Best wishes' the most common sign-offs. If in doubt use the more traditional 'Dear' and 'Yours sincerely' or if you want to be slightly less formal 'Dear' and 'Regards'. 'Love and kisses' is probably never appropriate in the workplace.

Avoid using emoticons

An emoticon is an electronic symbol of emotions. Most people don't understand what you mean. Recipients of emails, particularly in the working environment do become annoyed by emails that are overfamiliar or include spelling and grammatical errors. Remember, check before you send!

The use of different font and colours can be distracting

You want your email to be clear and easy to read so keep it simple.

The use of capitals in the main text of an email is the equivalent of shouting at somebody

Do not use them unless you would normally shout at the person if you were speaking face to face!

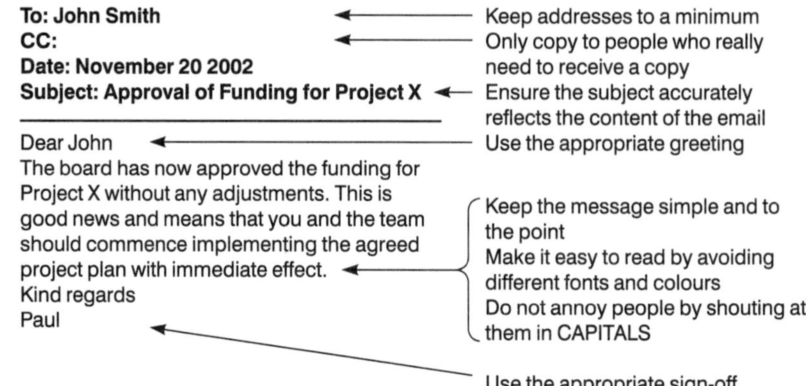

Figure 9.3 Writing the perfect email

Keep emails short

If they are equivalent to more than a sheet of A4 paper then use attachments. People easily get bored or distracted when reading long emails.

9.7 Case study of an email policy taken from a public sector organization

This shows an example of a relatively simple but effective email policy.

9.7.1 Email etiquette and protocols

The growth in the use of emails in the organization has brought with it some considerable advantages. Communication can now be timely – though we are all dependent on network capacity and performance. There is also considerably less paper passing around between departments in the form of memoranda.

There are also, however, downsides to this development. There is an increasing load on the network and on individuals' screens, comprising messages that are sent to colleagues, either on the off-chance that they might be interested, or because the sender feels that it would be a good idea for the recipient to know about a particular issue. Email communication can also on occasions be somewhat curt, which has led to some adverse comments from recipients, suggesting that more care needs to be taken over this form of communication.

We feel therefore, that it is appropriate to set out some general principles to cover the use of email within the organization. We have also taken the opportunity to give some guidance on the use of the organization's email addresses for private use.

Guidelines

Email is an easy form of communication but it is important that within the organization we try to keep some form of overall control if only to ensure that important messages are read in a timely fashion and irrelevant material does not impinge on an individual's workload. The following guidelines are therefore set out to try to avoid some of the worse pitfalls of email communication:

Remember that emails are part of the permanent record and you should take as much care over their content as any other written form of communication.

- *Try to ensure that emails are copied only to those people who have an immediate need to receive the information contained in the communication. Additional copies both waste colleagues' time and contribute to network overload.*
- *Use address groups whenever possible. Scrolling endless addresses is frustrating and not necessary.*
- *Return only that part of the original message that needs to be sent back – it's much easier for the reader if unnecessary material is edited from the return message. However, for those who receive many emails each day some reference to the original issue is important, so erasing all trace of the original message can be counterproductive.*
- *Use the subject field to be as specific as you can to assist the recipient to identify the issue being discussed quickly.*
- *Avoid long and detailed emails which will require excessive scrolling to read on-screen. Generally, anything above one side of A4 should probably be communicated in another format – probably by an attachment.*
- *Set out the email on the screen so that it is easily legible and conforms to reasonable standards of graphic presentation. Short paragraphs are very helpful to readers.*
- *Unless it is absolutely necessary, do not request a confirmation of delivery and reading, since this adds to the network traffic in an unnecessary way.*
- *Avoid including a full address for internal emails – particularly burdensome if it also includes a full international address, telephone number and personal homily.*

Personal emails

We recognize that many people receive and respond to personal emails through their work address. We expect that:

1 *such emails are kept short;*
2 *work addresses are not used for sending on 'chain emails';*
3 *work addresses are not used to communicate personal opinions or statements, for example to the press or as part of a private legal case where the use of the work email address could lead the recipient to attribute a personal view to this organization.*

9.8 Summary

This chapter has looked at emails as a modern form of communication and the challenges that communicating in emails presents both the individual and the organization. As a relatively new form of written communication we need to create guidelines for ensuring that we use emails both appropriately and effectively. The key points are summarized below.

Five ways to ensure email communication is appropriate and effective:

1 Think of emails as any other form of written communication.
2 Write the email from the reader's point of view and understanding.
3 Produce protocols and guidelines for emails as with any other form of written communication.
4 Ensure everybody in the organization is aware of, and sticks to, the policy.
5 Think before you press! Is email the best medium for this particular communication and is it going to make the impression you want.

10 Email on the move: a necessity or an option?

Do I really need access to my email all the time?
What are the benefits of being able to access my email when I am on the move?
What are the drawbacks of accessing my email in transit?

10.1 Introduction

This world offers a pretty sad, thin, painfully inadequate experience. I can't help feeling that access to this stuff isn't the big advantage they all think it is. I think the so-called data-rich may well turn out to be the losers: sad screen drones, plugging away with their mod cons and instant online access into an empty space because it happens down the phone line. In my world the privileged may well be the unplugged.

Janet Street-Porter, *Without Walls: J'Accuse-Tecnonerds*, Channel 4, 19 March 1996

Like everything to which one becomes addicted, we start to fret and worry when we cannot have our regular fix, be it a drink, a favourite food such as a marmite sandwich for breakfast, the newspaper or a round of golf. For many, not being able to access their email at all times represents just such a nightmare. Others, while genuinely not bothered, find themselves falling prey to the $24 \times 7 \times 365$ culture and an ethos that suggests that being able to deal with email anywhere, anyplace, anytime is the norm. Do you find yourself becoming sucked into the genre for email on-tap, which is being driven by a pincer movement of your colleagues and the technology industry? Have you started to feel like a leper because you don't have one of those smart devices that enable you to have your regular fix of email?

One day I (the author of this particular chapter) was travelling to a client organization with whom I would spend the day. I realized that I would have about an hour and a half free between meetings. The organization's office is remote from any shops and from my own office. Any 'downtime' has to be spent on their site. 'Drat,' I thought, 'if only I could access my email it would save having to set aside an hour this evening to deal with it.'

Then the rational part of my brain took over. What was I thinking about? Downtime is an opportunity to network and talk to the other directors and members of the organization. It is a chance to catch up on how they and their part of the business are doing and to sow the seed for some future work! (How much extra work is often generated by those casual corridor conversations and informal discussions?) And to think I nearly sacrificed quality time at one of my key clients for the sake of reading a few emails.

There are those of you for whom instant access to your email is critical to the job and role you perform, for example the European operation director of a global organization probably needs email on-tap. Likewise, a fund manager may need to know about important changes in the market, and a salesman and engineer who by the nature of their job are mobile and need to access their email on the move.

However, many of us have a choice: we can decide whether or not we deal with our email on the move. The information technology and communications industry is notorious for producing smart gadgets, which are driven by technological excellence but often fulfil no real business need. Remember the Sinclair C5 or the Apple Newton? Market pressure may make us feel that it is not optional whether we have one or not. While there are some interesting new devices that make it possible to access your email wherever you are (24×7×365 if necessary), don't let yourself be lured into believing it is compulsory. You are not 'sad' or odd if you only access your email when appropriate to your needs – you are a balanced individual who 'has a life', you don't need to have your finger in your inbox at all times.

In this chapter we will explore:

- reasons why you would want to access your email on the move;
- advantages and disadvantages of always having access to your inbox.

The choice of device to access your email is covered in the next chapter. The focus of both these chapters is about accessing your email when you are truly on the move, that is in transit between, say, different offices or meetings (rather than the need to access them from another fixed place such as home). The contents are designed to help those focusing on their own needs and those responsible for setting the corporate policy.

10.2 The case for email on the move

So what is the case for and against dealing with your email on the move?

10.2.1 Benefits

The principal advantages of instant access to your email anywhere, anytime are:

- staying in touch;
- being more responsive to the needs of others;
- keeping on top of the inbox;
- no backlog when you return to the office after being away for any length of time (even a day in meetings);
- staying in control;
- being able to micro-manage (if needs be);
- a way of communicating that complements your preferred management style and behaviour patterns, as discussed in previous chapters.

10.2.2 Disadvantages

Against this immediacy and feeling of staying in touch the major disadvantages of handling your inbox on the move are:

- another activity eating into time you might use for other tasks, e.g. thinking and reading;
- the need to carry extra clutter (i.e. devices and sometimes cables);
- the security risk;
- never quite switching off from the office especially if you are one of those who dips in and out of their email when on leave.

Accessing your email on the move raises security risks. These include the basic problem of losing or having your remote access device stolen, to the more serious problem of creating potentially weak links in your corporate computer network security systems. These issues are discussed in the next chapter.

Today, many of us feel that we really should be accessing our email even when we are on leave which, as Cary Cooper points out, means that we never have a proper break and learn to relax:

> *Accessing your email on holiday really is a no, no, no. We all need respite away from the distractions of doing business. We need quality time with our families and partners without worrying about work and letting it spill over into that time. If you open your email it will put you into a different frame of mind, especially if there is bad news. You will do less listening to the family and it will be just like being back at work.*
>
> *Let the office pick it up for you and only forward it to you if there really is a crisis. If there is one the chances are you will need other papers you don't have and be tempted to fly back home.*
>
> *Not opening your email when on leave sends a loud message that you are not a workaholic. Often, when I tell people I am going off-line they then start talking to me person-to-person, not role-to-role, and a richer relationship starts to develop as you get to know each other better. So here is an indirect benefit of being off-line from time to time to deal with the life part of the work–life balance.*
>
> Cary Cooper, BUPA Professor of Organizational Psychology and Health, University of Manchester Institute of Science and Technology

Those who do access their email would say that this is far better than returning to a full inbox and needing to spend the first few hours if not days catching up. But think back to the days of paper mail? How many of you had your paper in-tray forwarded to you on holiday? In any case, if you are starting to prune back your inbox and decrease the level of noise, as outlined earlier, then there should be far fewer to deal with after a break!

10.3 Do you need to access your email on the move?

This is a top question asked by many executives for whom remote access is a choice. It is also a major issue for those who may choose not to access their own email but who need to make decisions about how their business unit operates. The flow chart in Figure 10.1 is designed to help you make a decision about your own needs and, as appropriate, start thinking about a policy for your team.

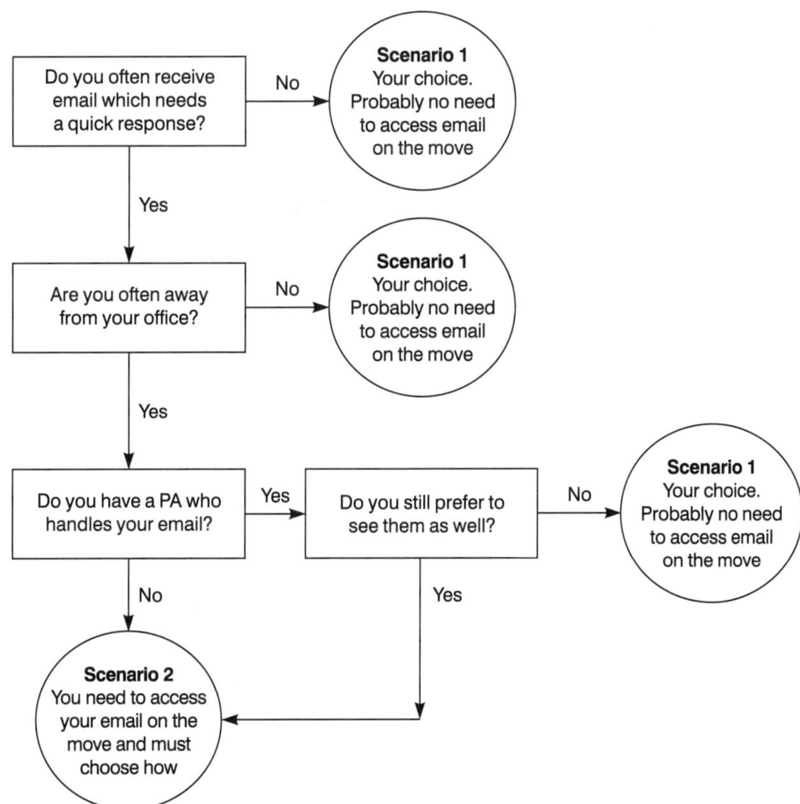

Figure 10.1
Do you need email on the move?

10.3.1 Scenario 1 – no real need to access your email on the move

This is the situation where you really **do have a choice** about whether or not you decide to access your email when you are away from the office and certainly on the move. The crunch is really the volume of 'urgent' emails that you receive, and whether or not you have someone who manages your inbox in your absence. By 'urgent' we mean 'action' type emails you must respond to, otherwise something will go amiss in the business (a client will be upset, a wrong decision made, etc.). This is opposed to the ones that the sender may perceive as urgent, but in reality can wait for a response and may even just be creating noise in your inbox.

Typically you are primarily based in one location. When you are away from your office, either in meetings or at another office you have ready access to your emails by logging-in to a terminal at another location. You may or may not have a secretary, PA or colleague who will deal with your inbox in your absence. If you do and you have a very good working relationship, you may be perfectly happy to delegate this responsibility to them. If you decide to deal with your inbox at home you will probably have a PC (laptop or desktop) through which you have to dial up access to the main server.

10.3.2 Scenario 2 – a real need to access your email on the move

This is the situation where you are probably spending a high proportion of your time out of your office perhaps in meetings within either your own organization or other organizations. The only way to keep on top of your email is to deal with it remotely, whether in a hotel or physically on the move. Crucially, a high proportion of the email you receive does require a quick, often immediate response, if your part of the business is to function effectively with instant responses. Typically you might be head of a global business unit, operations director or a consultant.

Now your main question is what type of device should you use, and this is explored in detail after the case histories.

10.4 Case histories

These three case histories highlight the different ways people work and why for some the choice is not to bother with lugging around any mobile email technology.

10.4.1 Case history – Christine, marketing director, engineering company

Christine is out about two days a week, and has developed a very good working relationship with Sarah her PA, who handles her email in her absence. While Christine receives about 40 emails per day, few need an instant response. When they do Sarah phones her to discuss them and then either Sarah responds or more usually Christine responds by phone. She accesses her inbox from home either in the evening or at weekends when there really is a need.

This is a Scenario 1 situation. Accessing her email on the move would probably not add any significant extra value for Christine in terms of how she runs her part of the business and manages herself.

10.4.2 Case history – John, chief operating officer, telecommunications company

John commutes one hour each way from home to office and back. He is a gold user and part of his business is looking for new ways that his company can exploit mobile telecommunications. He does not have a PA and few of his emails need an instant response. But he just enjoys using technology and chooses to deal with his inbox while he commutes.

This too is an example of Scenario 1, but John has made the choice to deal with his inbox while on the move. He feels it adds value for him – otherwise he would be faced with spending an hour each night clearing his inbox at home.

10.4.3 Case history – Julie, European HR director, global food manufacturer

Many of Julie's emails need a quick response from her, sometimes a straight yes to attend a meeting, and often a holding response while she works out how to solve a problem. Her PA deals with her email but Julie likes to see it all at the end of the day

Julie needs email on tap wherever she is and needs to be able to deal with it on the move between meetings and while in transit.

This is the Scenario 2 situation. Julie has no choice – her job demands that she is always on call and in touch with the organization.

10.5 Summary – what's best for me?

> **How else can I spend my time?**
> - How do I currently use my time in transit?
> - How important is it that I continue to do these tasks (e.g. reading, meetings, checking papers, thinking, maybe even just relaxing)?
> - When else will there be time for me to do those tasks?

Are you contemplating dealing with your email on the move as you travel between meetings and clients? The key is to be clear that doing so either adds value to your preferred way of working or the work you are doing. If you **choose to board the 'on the move' email** gravy train just ask yourself the boxed questions.

So if you still want to access your email on the move, what are the options? Chapter 11 provides an overview of the different options available to you.

11 Ways to access your email on the move

How easy is it to handle my email when I am in transit?
What are the problems about mobile email access?
What is the best way for me?

11.1 Introduction

For those who either need or choose to access their email on the move there is a bewildering choice as to which device to use – from handheld to conventional laptop to dedicated 'always-on' pager type devices. Then you have to choose the right form of communications to suit your way of working, for example wireless, a phone linked to a PC and so on.

The dilemma for most of us is what device to choose. Do we opt for a device primarily for email or one piece of equipment that will act as both a phone and an email carrier – a convergent device?

The search for a convergent device that can handle both voice and data communications with equal effectiveness still has the air of the search for the Holy Grail. New equipment has been and continues to be launched as a never-ending stream of choice. We, the users, are both the beneficiaries and the unwitting prey of the PC and the telecommunications manufacturers.

The mobile communications industry is probably the fastest and most exciting part of the whole PC and communications technology market place. All the players, be they hardware, software, communications manufacturers or suppliers, are vying for market share and trying to develop the one '*absolute must have!* gadget'. Take a look at any newspaper over a week and just monitor the news items relating to remote email access. There are usually over five items a week, covering everything from new devices to ever faster and cheaper access times.

The merit and suitability of any option depends entirely on the purpose for which you need them. As always there is a trade-off between functionality (i.e. range of functions the device can perform) and size, which is likely to remain constant for at least the foreseeable future. That is:

Functionality is directly proportional to size and cost – and inversely proportional to ease of use!

You also have a choice about how you interact with your email, from conventional keyboard input to speech recognition. Intimately linked to what device you choose is the question of what communications protocol (method of access) you should use, from conventional modems to Wi-Fi.

This chapter contains an overview and comparison of the:

- different ways of accessing email remotely (devices and communications protocols);
- advantages and disadvantages of the various methods for accessing email on the move.

Lastly, there is a grid to help you choose which options might be best for you.

11.2 Range of devices

The devices for handling your email on the move fall into four broad categories:

- Smart phones
- Handheld computers
- Laptops
- Dedicated devices

11.2.1 Terminology

Just a word on terminology: the information and communications technology (ICT) industry has been, and will probably continue to be, a shining example of the 'emperor's new clothes' syndrome. New words are invented to describe old phenomena in the hope of selling new technology. A mobile device that is capable of handling data and voice is often called a personal digital assistant (PDA). This term was coined in the late 1980s by Apple and Psion to describe their early ventures into this market place. However, there are now several terms that are used to describe different types of PDA-like devices.

Personal digital assistant (PDA)

This term is used here generically to describe those devices, be they phones or handheld PCs, which can handle and help you manage a combination of data-based information such as email, address books, and electronic diary.

Smart phones

A mobile phone with PIM (Personal Information Manager) capabilities such as an electronic diary, and contact management.

Communicator

Nokia's trade name to describe their smart phone.

Handheld

A small palm-sized PC-based PDA which may handle either data only or data and voice (i.e. be convergent).

Palmtop

The same as a handheld, the phrase being coined after Palm, who have been one of the leaders in this sector of the market.

All these terms really have much the same connotation. Just as some of us refer to a vacuum cleaner as either a Hoover or a Dyson (after two of the leading manufactures of these goods) so the names of these personal digital assistant devices are often used interchangeably. For the purpose of this chapter we will use the terms 'handheld' to refer to small palm-sized PC-based devices and 'smart phone' to refer to those devices which are mobile phone based.

All these PDA devices offer a certain basic level of functionality, which includes some or all of the following:

- email management;
- electronic diary;
- to-do lists;
- contact database;
- note pad.

Some offer additional functionality such as:

- access to Microsoft-based applications and files such as spreadsheets, documents and presentations;
- internet access;
- games.

The following sections provide an overview of the main differences between the different types of devices.

11.2.2 Smart phones

As their name suggests, these look and feel like conventional mobile phones but may have added capability to handle email and provide other functionality such as an electronic diary, contact management, to-do list, word processing and spreadsheet capability. Manufacturers in this space include Nokia with its Communicator range of phones, Sony, Ericsson, Samsung, Motorola and Kyocera. Some tend to be about twice as heavy as a conventional dedicated mobile phone (e.g. Nokia Communicator), but others with a small screen are simply very functional normal mobile phones. In making a choice you trade off physical size (particularly the screen) for user convenience.

11.2.3 Handhelds

Currently, these essentially come in four flavours according to their ability to be used as a phone, and the operating system on which they are based, as summarized in Figure 11.1. There are those which are single purpose PC look-alike devices without integrated phone capability (e.g. Compaq iPAQ) and those which are multipurpose as supplied (convergent) and can therefore also be used as a mobile phone out of the box (Handspring Treo and XDA from O_2).

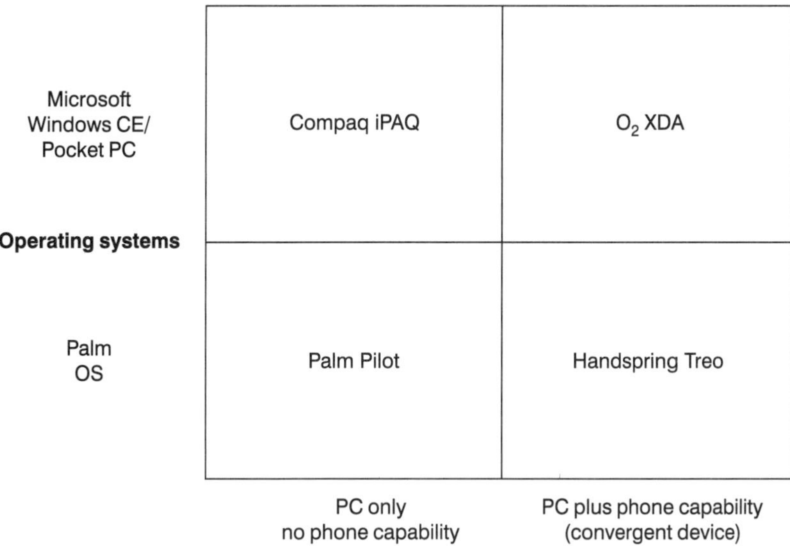

Figure 11.1 Handheld PCs – variations on a theme

All work in the same way in terms of enabling you to synchronize the contents of your inbox, electronic diary and contacts database from your main PC to and from your handheld. You can synchronize at any point in time and hence deal with your inbox and other mail folders through both your PC or handheld. That is you can read existing emails and compose replies and new ones while on the move. In essence synchronization gives you a common snapshot of your inbox (and electronic diary, etc.) at that point.

However, in order to send and receive email on the move, you either need one which has built in wireless (GSM or GPRS today) connectivity (such as the XDA or Handspring Treo) or an add-on phone/modem (such as the wireless Nokia Card Phone 2 which fits the iPAQ (with a replicator sleeve)). This lets you dial up (as you would with a mobile phone) and send and receive new email. Alternatively, if your handheld does not have or can't achieve this integrated wireless capability you can either connect by linking the PDA to your mobile phone (via cable or infrared, where the phone acts both as modem and access link to the cellular network) or wait until you reach your office and resynchronize the handheld with your main PC and send them that way. (We'll talk about Bluetooth later, but note for now that some phones and PDAs can use this short-distance radio technology instead of cable or infrared.)

11.2.4 Windows CE, Palm OS or EPOC?

To perplex users even further there are several basic operating systems used to power handhelds, including Microsoft's Windows CE (Consumer Electronics), Palm OS from 3COM who developed the Palm Pilot family of handhelds, and Epoc which is well known on the Psion series of PDAs and is also used by some phone manufacturers. These operating systems afford much the same functionality. The main difference, as you would imagine, is that those based on Windows Pocket PC offer an environment more familiar to Windows users, through the provision of a cut-down version of Windows and Office called Pocket PC. Speed and convenience of synchronization vary but generally the Palm is reckoned to be the most bulletproof, with Pocket PC offering a more familiar user interface. Just realize that *none* of these operating systems actually bears any relation to the code that supports PCs; the operating hardware of the handhelds is very different and all the manufacturers' code bases for handhelds are specialized to that family. Just because a device's screen looks like other offerings from a functionality perspective means nothing in terms of code maturity.

For smart phones the choice is between Windows CE or Epoc from the Symbian consortium, or the Palm OS suite of applications. Again, what the manufacturer has done under the covers to make it work will be very different for each brand.

Again those handhelds that are convergent are heavier and often cumbersome: and although it can be done, it is not very convenient to access data from the PC part while on the phone as the one device does everything. There is no separate handset, although they generally have a hands-free earplug appliance that also doubles as a microphone (like the hands-free earplug that you can attach to a conventional mobile phone) and sometimes a speaker. There are several subtle differentiators between smart phones and handheld devices as summarized in Table 11.1.

Perhaps the most significant difference is the extent of the ability to synchronize the handheld or phone to the contents of your main PC (be it a laptop or desktop machine). Smart-phones will 'sync' your inbox, and contact information, and even calendar, but not usually specific files you may want to carry with you. For documents, simple spreadsheets and even limited presentations, you generally need a handheld. Indeed

Table 11.1 Comparison of handhelds, smart phones and laptops

Factor	Handheld PC	Smart phone	Laptop
Synchronize with your main PC	Yes, but you may not be able to access all your email folders.	Limited.	Yes, and have full access to all email folders through your network mail server.
Handling attachments	Varies, can be limited, may not be able to receive them.	Very limited.	Not an issue.
Network access	Depends on model, may be limited to one access method.	Often limited to phone network provider/carrier.	Flexible, can use multiple methods and carriers.
Ways of inputting data	Multiple, speech handwriting or keyboard.	Limited mainly keyboard, like SMS.	Multiple.
Screen size and clarity	Small, portrait shape, top models have excellent screen resolution, but some can be hard to read in bright light. Some can do landscape.	Small, landscape shape, often not as easy to read.	Full laptop size screen with the best resolution and the easiest to read in all conditions.
Size of keyboard	Smaller, but can attach larger size keyboard.	A little larger than handhelds, may not be able to attach larger one.	Full.
Functionality	Depends on manufacturer.	Same as handheld.	Full functionality.
Expandability	Can add peripherals (e.g. keyboard) and often extra memory and software.	Limited.	Unlimited.
Weight	Generally lighter than a laptop, but weight depends on model.	Lighter than handhelds.	Heavier than handheld or smart phone, but the lightest is only 1.2 kg.
Battery life	Limited, depends on purpose and extent to which you you use it; colour is biggest consumer!	Longer.	Limited and less than most handhelds.

with the right software you can review and run a presentation through a handheld. As one ardent user commented:

> *This is a bonus because when I am on the train, although I cannot edit the presentation, I can rehearse the words and timing.*
>
> Tony, director of operations, government agency

Clearly the functionality and specification will depend on both the manufacturer and model. The pace at which this sector of the ICT industry is changing means factors such as battery life, screen resolution and size can only improve for the benefit of us, the users. Bear in mind that bright colour screens are great, even outdoors, but eat batteries.

11.2.5 Laptops

As laptops become ever smaller in the form of a 'notebook' PC these are still the preferred option for many mainly because they offer the full functionality of a PC. The lightest notebooks now weigh about 1.2 kg and some are less than 2.5 cm thick.

11.3 Handling your emails

As indicated in the introduction and in Table 11.1, there are a variety of ways by which you can interact with your emails and these include:

- keyboard;
- 'Graffiti';
- handwriting recognition;
- voice activation.

11.3.1 Keyboard

Keyboard interaction can be through a:

- built-in 'soft' keyboard which you tap with a stylus;
- small built-in keypad which you work with either finger or thumbs (key feature of Blackberry and the Treo with keyboard option); some have miniature add-on keyboards;
- full size keyboard, which you can attach to the device (these usually fold up for convenience and mobility).

11.3.2 'Graffiti'

This is a trade mark of the 'Palm'-based handheld PC devices. You enter text through symbols using a stylus. It is actually easier and quicker to learn and use than it sounds. Interestingly, Microsoft's Pocket PC 2002 has recognized this and now offers a facility like this as one of its four screen input options.

11.3.3 Handwriting recognition

Some of the newer handheld PC devices can recognize your handwriting. While this can be slower and more prone to errors it is an alternative for those who do not feel comfortable with a keyboard or 'Graffiti'.

11.3.4 Voice activation

This can be achieved either directly through the device, if it has the capability, or using a specialist device such as the Sony Memory Stick solid-state recorder:

> *One of the major advantages of this approach is that one can dictate directly oneself, and hand the memory stick over to a personal assistant who can correct documents/top and tail etc. without having to go through the laborious typing process from start to finish.*
>
> Phil, managing consultant, international consultancy practice

The choice is largely yours, and really it is about finding a way that suits when and how you prefer to work.

11.4 Connectivity

Having chosen your device how do you connect with the outside world to send and receive emails? First and foremost there is the traditional and now conventional way of accessing your email via a modem through either a landline at the place to which you have travelled (e.g. a hotel, another office) or via your mobile phone (using its 'soft' modem). For those wanting to handle their email on the move here are four main options:

- GSM via a mobile
- GPRS
- Wi-Fi
- 3G

11.4.1 GSM

You link your device to your server via dial-up through a mobile phone device. The main downside is low speed (9.6–14.4 Kbps) and variable quality of the signal from your network provider. If you lose the connection you have to start over again.

11.4.2 GPRS

General Packet Radio Services (GPRS) is becoming increasingly popular. It is a wireless protocol, running over the same cellular network that GSM employs. It enables you to send data communications over your mobile phone network at a faster speed than GSM (generally about five times faster). GPRS is sometimes called 2.5G in terms of speed and richness of text and images which you can download from the internet, from either WAP or otherwise adapted sites. Most new PDA devices (handhelds and smart phones) are GPRS enabled. You can buy a GPRS enabled card to use in your laptop (or handheld if it is not GPRS enabled) and then connect to your chosen service provider, of which there are several.

Although both GPRS and GSM are reliant on good reception and hence prone to falling over, it is much less annoying with GPRS because if you are in the middle of downloading a large email and it fails, it will automatically re-establish the transmission where it left off. Technically, being packet based it is a 'connectionless' technology, unlike GSM which is connection oriented, requiring a permanently reserved connection for each session. GPRS enables much more productivity on trains – we have all experienced the tunnel effect!

11.4.3 Wi-Fi

This is relatively new and fast becoming very popular. A very local form of local area networking (LAN) like Bluetooth (but better) it enables you to connect cable-free through a Wi-Fi network server, router or peer-to-peer network (assuming you have a Wi-Fi network card or built-in functionality in your PC). In essence you piggy-back on to the server for fast connectivity to your desired services, which is by and large robust and less prone to falling over especially due to poor reception as is encountered with GPRS and GSM. Many places are now linked up for Wi-Fi (e.g. stations, coffee shops and professional membership clubs such as the Institute of Directors). Wi-Fi networks are becoming increasingly common in organizations and at home. While 3G may be designed to be the fastest way to access data through cellular national and international services (e.g. smart phones and convergent multipurpose handhelds), Wi-Fi will and should continue to offer fast access to data dominant devices such as handheld PDAs and tablet PCs on a *local* basis, linking through the server for other services such as the internet.

Also known as 802.11b wireless Ethernet, Wi-Fi now works at 11 Mbps, faster than the original 1.6 Mbps and much faster than Bluetooth. Microwave ovens can still cause interference, and of course you must stay in range of the Wi-Fi connection point. Be sure to use the optional 128-bit encryption – passers-by can access your wireless protocol if you don't. You may even find chalk marks on the street outside your home or office thoughtfully provided by those in the know for others to cash in on your unprotected network! (A practice known as 'warchalking – see below.)

Warchalking

Wi-Fi has generated a unique security problem. With a Wi-Fi enabled device it is possible to access someone else's network. This has given rise to ardent mobile users initiating a 'warchalking' code of practice. They draw chalk marks on buildings and pavements to denote buildings with Wi-Fi nodes. The practice is based on a similar one used by American tramps during the American depression to indicate where they had been lucky to find shelter or food. Warchalkers have even developed their own 'hobo-language' to denote the type of access you can expect.

Warchalker's 'hobo-language'	
Symbol	**Meaning**
Two back-to-back semicircles	an open node
A circle	a closed node
W	a wireless equivalent protocol

Although, the main telecom and internet service providers are trying to outlaw the practice there is little doubt that it will persist. Indeed, we may see a similar battle between the telcos and warchalkers as we see between ramblers and landowners, especially since the warchalkers have now formalized themselves into a group with their own website (www.warchalking.org). Co-operating neighbours have even utilized this opportunity to share cable operator costs through a domestic Wi-Fi router in one of the houses.

11.4.4 3G

This is the much-heralded next generation for mobile phone connectivity. It will enable you to access your email and a whole range of other multimedia information much faster (e.g. full internet services, video and music). For example, at the time of writing the current MMS (Multimedia Message Service) facility in some smart phones is not supported by some network operators. With 3G, such multimedia (image and voice) messaging will be fast and easy.

11.4.5 Bluetooth

Bluetooth is a protocol that allows you to make a wireless connection from your PC device to many other items of PC equipment such as printers, handhelds, phones, hands-free sets and LAN networks. It will enable you to connect your mobile phone to your PC device providing both are 'Bluetooth enabled'. Increasingly both handheld and smart phones are being released which are already bluetooth enabled. Thus it offers yet another mobile way of accessing your emails. For example you can synchronize your PDA with your main PC and hence collect your emails when walking around your office (if you really want to!). Similarly you could access a network in a building which is Bluetooth enabled. In some ways it is in direct competition to Wi-Fi and it remains to be seen which becomes the *de facto* standard.

11.4.6 Round-up

The speed of connectivity and richness of data afforded by these different methods are summarized in Figure 11.2. If you work for an organization, the method you choose will be dictated by the corporate information systems (IS strategy). For those who work for themselves and are just venturing into this arena, the

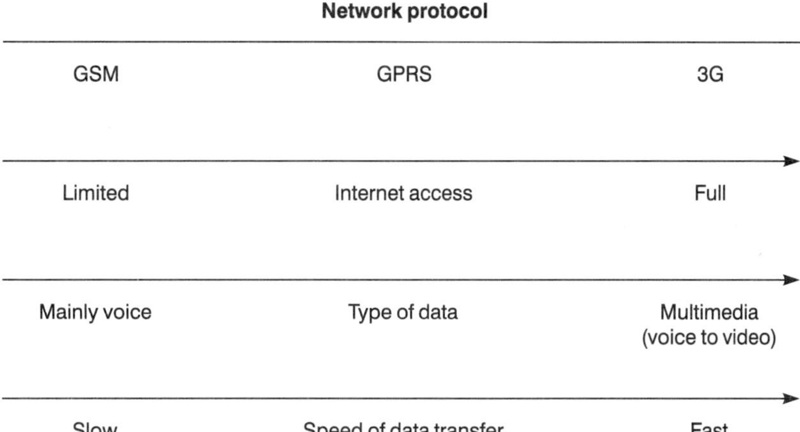

Figure 11.2
Comparison of network protocols

choice will depend on what you really need, cost and your existing hardware policy and infrastructure. Some questions to help you decide are to be found at the end of this chapter.

With all these methods of connectivity you must first make a connection through your chosen network protocol. None gives you instant access to new email in the same way as you would get if you were in your office connected to a network (e.g. through Microsoft Exchange or Lotus Notes). For truly instant remote access that is 'always on' you need a dedicated device such as Blackberry.

11.4.7 Blackberry

Blackberry is a small PDA type device that is 'always on' through its connectionless packet-based GPRS protocol. It can notify you of new mail by either bleeping or vibrating just like a pager. Blackberry is very much state of the art as Brian Sutton, director of IS for 'learndirect', comments: 'this is the vision of the future'. You do not need to dial up or find a Wi-Fi point. Blackberry just delivers your email to your Blackberry pager and there it sits ready for when you are ready to deal with it. It provides a truly wireless instant email service (working through O_2's GPRS network). In a way it's like SMS messaging (which it also provides) in terms of always being connected, but of course with the much richer facilities of email. You don't dial anyone to keep in touch, you just send and receive and GPRS packet management does the rest.

The device is not much bigger than a pack of cards. The keyboard is designed to be used with your two thumbs as you hold it in your fingers. It has an electronic calendar, which is also always synchronized with your office diary and the usual other PIM facilities.

Users of Blackberry all cite advantages, which include:

- being more productive in terms of being able to respond more quickly;
- no waiting to find a connection to send and receive emails;
- absolutely up-to-date calendar;
- improved work–life balance.

> *It has given me back my Sundays. I like to log-on on Sundays to check my email. With a laptop that might take five to ten minutes and I would then get sucked into doing other things. With Blackberry it takes me five to ten seconds and I am up to speed.*
>
> Rob, programme director of a major telecommunications organization

Like most such mobile devices accessing attachments is not straightforward and you often need to do a bit of jiggery-pokery to deceive Blackberry. For example, you must have them sent either within the body of the email or to another device/person who can access attachments. Blackberry offer an email address to which you can send an email with an attachment and you receive it back – normally within a minute – with the attachment in the email body. Another advantage is that if you want to forward an email to someone, the attachment need never come to your Blackberry – it goes straight from server to server, whatever kind of file it is.

So what is the catch? Why is everyone who wants instant access to email not using Blackberry, which has been described by many as the 'must have' gadget. Blackberry is an enterprise solution aimed at the large corporates who use Microsoft Exchange. This is because the service is provided through an attached Blackberry server and for this you need deep pockets. For a 20-user system you could be looking at a capital outlay of £11 500 plus running costs of £780 per month. (The Blackberry pager currently costs about £450 per user, a 20-user licence about £2500 and about £40 per month for the airtime.) But for any organization wanting their own GPRS services, providing high(er) speed email services remotely to their staff, this is the kind of future we are looking at.

11.4.8 Other options

Last but by no means least there are two other options for those who want access to their whole email system while away from the office but do not wish to carry a laptop: a wireless modem like the Sierra AirCard and GoToMyPC.

Sierra AirCard

These essentially require a wireless modem, which comprises a smart card and antennae to your laptop, and subscribe to an appropriate mobile data provider like Vodaphone. In essence this is the small organization's solution to Blackberry as it offers 'always on' access to your email. Suppliers include Sierra (www.sierra.com) and Novatel (www.Novatel.com).

GoToMyPC

For this you merely download the GoToMyPC software (from www.GoToMyPC.com) and install it on your main office PC which contains your master email program and files and then subscribe to the GoToMyPC service. This then enables you to access your personal host machine from anywhere in the world through the internet. (If you are using Microsoft Exchange you can do something similar.) It also enables you have your emails forwarded to any worldwide ISP account, but GoToMyPC is a simpler option which has proved popular among smaller businesses:

> *On a recent trip to a client in the USA I needed to access some old emails and other files but I had decided not to take my PC. Using GoToMyPC meant I could easily do this without having to wait for someone (my wife in my case) to access the files for me. I just took control of the PC as if I was in the office.*
>
> Sam, founder and principal consultant of a small IT consultancy practice

11.4.9 On the horizon

Keeping pace with the latest developments and buying a state of the art device is like chasing after the end of the rainbow. There are undoubtedly many developments on or just over the horizon. Some will solve existing problems such as speed of access and the functionality versus size dichotomy. Already there is much talk about the end of the PC as we know it.

As we write, the first 'Tablet' PCs have just been launched. These will look and feel like a pad of paper and be capable of enabling you to access your email on the move via a range of protocols from modems to Wi-Fi. You will be able to deal with them using both conventional handwriting and a keyboard.

Moreover, in an effort to generate more sales and create market share, there is no doubt that the price of these PDA type devices will drop and their functionality will increase (in a pattern like Moore's law for processor speeds, memory and disc capacity). In September 2002 Palm announced a new model (the Zire), which will sell for just £70 and come with Bluetooth and GPRS.

11.5 Security

All mobile devices carry a security warning (like the health warning on a cigarette packet), not least because such objects from laptops to smart phones are highly desirable: the smaller and more 'state of the art' the more desirable. Apart from the cost and inconvenience of losing your PDA other hidden costs include:

- loss of valuable (often confidential) corporate information;
- loss of critical personal data (e.g. bank account numbers);
- access by intruders to the corporate network.

In addition some PDA operating platforms seem more prone to harbouring viruses than others although no doubt all the manufacturers will eventually tighten up this area.

Interestingly, and perhaps because PDAs were first seen as very much personal and not part of the standard corporate computer pack, many IT departments had no real security polices for PDAs. However, that is slowly changing to the extent that some organizations will only allow you to use the standard issue of PDA. In an attempt to control how they are used, some companies also demand that synchronization must be direct with the company server rather than through the cradle that comes with the PDA.

Most IT departments are becoming more security conscious and are starting to implement a PDA security policy which includes guidelines about:

- what data can and cannot be accessed;
- which models are acceptable;

- level of security, which should be observed, such as using encryption for emails, and having anti-virus and firewall software installed.

11.5.1 What can you do to limit the security risk?

Five easy ways to protect your PDA

1. Never leave it lying around (however safe you think it might be).
2. Abide by the company's PDA security policy (and if one doesn't exist, initiate one).
3. Always password protect access to the software on your device (just as you should for a PC).
4. Never plug your device into an unknown machine.
5. Install anti-virus (and possibly firewall) software.

Apart from the obvious tips and hints such as not leaving devices lying around, here are five tips to help you protect yourself and your company's data assets from being stolen and save yourself all the stress that goes with this kind of theft. In this way, at least if the device is stolen you may be able to protect the data.

If you handle highly sensitive emails you should consider (or at least find out if the company demands that you use) encryption.

This is really just a very brief overview of some of the issues and solutions to protecting both the PDA and its contents. Your IT department should have more information. If they don't, hopefully this has given you enough to start a conversation about formulating the PDA security policy.

11.6 In reality – case histories

Certainly mobile access can be a minefield which the unwary would be wise to avoid unaided by an IT professional, unless you know exactly what you want. Here are two case histories that show different ways of using all the available technology to its best.

11.6.1 Case history – Simon, chief technology officer, telecommunications company

Simon is a gold level user and is a self-confessed 'email junkie'. He has a one-hour commute to work each way each day. He spends most of his time in the office very often in meetings. He has chosen to deal with his email when he travels between home and work. He has tried several small handheld devices but prefers a laptop, which he then connects over a conventional landline when he arrives at his destination:

I live by email. Everything is archived on my PC. To be truly productive I need to access my whole email inbox, that is all the subfolders and attachments, i.e. everything. Take today, I have over 100 emails which I will work my way through on the train tonight and file as I deal with them. I will also work on a client proposal if there is time.

I do occasionally use a handheld if I only want to deal with the really urgent ones and reply to them. But the screen is too small and the functionality limited. You can't download attachments easily or access your whole inbox filing system for old emails. They are very much here and now devices and less intrusive than a laptop.

A laptop is my preferred equipment, which I can then connect through my GPRS network at home. I used to send them via a mobile phone. But when you start to get half of Dixon's out of your brief case people start to stare at you.

11.6.2 Case history – Tony, operations director, government agency

Tony is a responsible email citizen and operates at the gold level of IT fitness. He travels extensively and rarely spends more than a day a week totally in the office:

Lots of the email I get needs an immediate response. Anyway, I like to deal with my email expeditiously. I don't like to let it mount up. Dealing with my email on the move is a great way to save time. Otherwise if I just rely on the phone we all waste time playing phone ping-pong.

I currently use a Blackberry device because it lets me be responsive and adaptive. Yes, there is a tendency for me to get involved with too much (when I read my emails) so I try to distance myself from emails that are not my responsibility. But I like to get things done.

The Blackberry is an immediate device, like sending SMS messages, but it is much more flexible because it has a full qwerty keyboard and I can use it as a phone if I need to. But it is not so good for attachments, so recently I have tried an 'XDA' handheld for the rare occasions when I need to handle those, e.g. work on a Word/Excel file. First I look at the email on my Blackberry, then decide if I need the attachment. Usually for Word documents I send it to Blackberry's website and have it returned in the body of the mail. Thanks to emerging GPRS agreements with overseas PTTs, both devices work in some European countries like Spain, for example. However, the USA still requires the third GSM frequency (1900 MHz) and so the triband phone or landline is still needed there to use browser mail via an ISP.

These things are not always as easy to connect as the suppliers would have you believe so it does help to have a technical background. And you do need to be careful about what you delete as you can find yourself losing emails when you go to synchronize the handheld with your main PC (especially on POP3 protocol used by some older devices).

But working like this suits me. It's my preferred way of working as it doesn't intrude on other people's way of working.

Both Tony and Simon are really gold plus users and both have probably tried every different type of device on the market, partly because they are interested in technology and partly because their jobs involve delivering services over the internet.

While we do not all need to have multiple devices, what these case histories show is just how different devices suit different people. Which device(s) you choose to access your email on the move really depends on your work styles and personal preferences as 'one size does not fit all'. Indeed we are very likely to want to use different devices for different situations – a point highlighted in a recent report from QNB Intelligence 'Corporate Wireless Adoption in Europe':

Right now, we are at the early stages in the evolution of the corporate wireless data marketplace . . . It is perfectly legitimate, for example to provide a professional user with Wireless LAN access to email on the Notebook PC for use in hotel rooms and GPRS access for on the train. They might also be provided with a wireless PDA for non-intrusive information access during customer meetings and monitoring of their inbox for important messages between meetings when booting up a PC is prohibitively inconvenient. Access from their pocketable WAP phone might be reserved for those 'off duty' times when they don't want to carry lots of gadgets but need to monitor their messages because an important deal is going on.

IBM Insight Report 'Corporate Wireless Adoption in Europe', QNB Intelligence

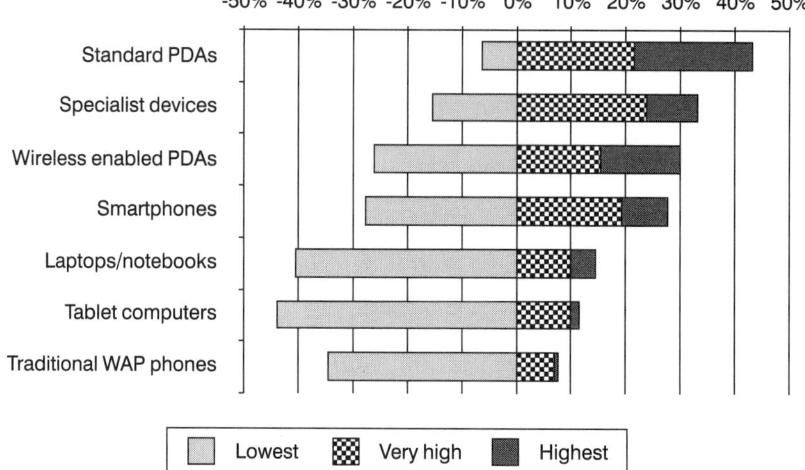

Figure 11.3 Trends in corporate wireless adoption. (From 'Corporate Wireless Adoption in Europe', QNB Intelligence, 2002)

11.7 Summary

These are just some of the many devices and ways in which you can now access your email on the move. Which one you choose will depend on many factors and as Adam Oliver of BT said 'we are all individuals and to some extent it is what suits your personality'.

We have provided tables comparing each option (devices and communications protocols) as they stand now. The market is moving so fast, that the latest fastest gizmo on some people's list of 'must have today' will be cast in sepia and heading for the technology graveyard by tomorrow. Another option is a checklist of questions to ask yourself to highlight your needs and then use to benchmark the available options against.

11.7.1 What's best for me?

Consider each item in the 'My mobile email checklist' opposite. To help you identify what are the most important functions and features for you, rank the relative importance. For example, give each one a weighting out of six using the following scale.

Importance	Weighting
Essential	6
Very useful	5
Useful	4
Nice to have	3
Not bothered	2
No perceived need	1

My mobile email list	
Selection criteria	**Importance**
Do I need to be able to access:	
• my full inbox files structure (i.e. all my email files)	
• attachments	
• other Office applications, e.g. Word files	
• a full keyboard	
• other methods of inputting data, e.g. voice and handwriting	
• the internet in full	
• international coverage	
• extra memory	
• add-on peripherals	
• Wi-Fi	
• Bluetooth	
• a built-in camera	
Is weight a factor?	
Do I need to comply with my organization's preferred platform (operating system) and device?	

This will help you build up a specification for a device, which meets your needs and helps you sift your way through the plethora of equipment on offer. If as is likely you are left with more than one possible candidate, last but by no means least ask yourself:

- Which device feels most comfortable for me?
- Which device suits me, my work style and (most importantly) my image?

By now you should have a very short list of acceptable options and the final choice may just come down to cost and availability. Availability should include not just the main device but also any essential add-ons. 'I am still waiting after two months for the spare chargers for my XDA', commented Brian Sutton, director of IS for 'learndirect'. As a real road warrior and heavy user of email on the move this is not just a 'nice to have' but an 'essential' for someone like him.

Part Three The corporate perspective

Security – it's not an IT problem; it's a business risk.
Computer Weekly, 14 September 2000

There is no question that email is here to stay and has permeated nearly every organizational process from welcoming new employees to responding to a client enquiry. The average time we spend dealing with our inboxes is between one and two hours. Clearly, as we have seen, this will vary according to how dependent our job is on email. If you have worked your way diligently through Parts One and Two of this book, you may have reduced the time you spend on email by up to 40 per cent. Is there scope to save more time? Or is it a fact of life that as the volume of email increases so you will need to spend even longer working your inbox?

It only takes one click . . .

With email it only takes a millisecond to destroy a brand image or precious relationship. Each week there are reports of some organization or another being sued for the inappropriate use of email. Examples to date include Norwich Union, Merrill Lynch, Credit Suisse, First Boston, Morgan Stanley, Microsoft and government agencies. Directors seethe at the way their employees have irresponsibly used email and damaged their organizations' brand image. Employees meanwhile complain bitterly about the time they have to spend on their inbox and the way their employers are scrutinizing their inbox. They were only having fun they retort, just like they used to joke around the coffee machine, but with email every word is recorded for reuse at a tribunal.

Who is really being irresponsible? A survey of HR directors in May 2002 by Mesmo Consultancy revealed that only 38 per cent thought their organization had an email code of best practice, and only 15 per cent of these directors thought anyone knew anything about it. This is because it is 'buried' among lots of other policies usually only brought to employees' attention when they join the company or if they face disciplinary action.

A recent survey by the American ePolicy Institute revealed that while 81 per cent of companies had a policy in place for internet and email use, only 51 per cent asked for any formal acknowledgement from employees that they had read the policy and only 24 per cent had taken any measure to train employees in how to comply with it.

Not so long ago a common element of any corporate management and development course included training on how to write letters and answer the phone. But how many of you include handling email in your business training, let alone include it in induction training?

Even in organizations that have decided to implement a policy the picture is somewhat hazy. For example, what does the policy contain? Who is responsible for it? Often it is left to the HR department, for after all this is a people issue isn't it? Sometimes it is the IT department, for after all isn't email something to do with technology? What organizations seem to overlook is that today, email is often the first point of contact between it and its potential customers in the outside world. Establishing email best practice should involve HR, IT, marketing and corporate communications (but specifically whoever is responsible for the company's communications policy including its image and reputation management).

Does your organization have an email policy, which is publicly available, promoted and enforced?

An email policy may tell you the purpose for which you can and cannot use email, but does it tell you anything about how to manage your inbox and behave towards other email users. We distinguish between email policy and email best practice:

- An explicit email policy (often called the **'netiquette' policy**) is about how and the purposes for which email should and should not be used.

- A code of acceptable behaviours – we call the **'good email citizen's charter'** – is a code of best practice that covers how to manage yourself and how to behave towards others.

In addition to the visible waste (e.g. time) and distress, there are a number of reasons why you would and should manage how email is used across the organization. These include:

- reducing time spent reading irrelevant emails generated by spam;
- protecting against spam and virus attacks;
- losing key corporate data;
- risking legal action for libellous content;
- conserving network resources;
- complying with government legislation such as the Data Protection Act, the Human Rights Act and the Regulation of Investigatory Powers Act.

The cost of email misuse – some facts and figures

- Meta Group estimates that between 2 and 10 per cent of all inbound corporate email can be classified as spam and that volume is expected to grow to 10–20 per cent during the next five years.
- One 5 Mb attachment file of jokes or pornography needs the same bandwidth as 160 normal text-based emails.
- Norwich Union paid £450 000 plus costs to a competitor as a result of circulating rumours about the competitor.
- Chevron (the US petrol company) paid £1.5 billion to an employee who was sexually harassed by email.
- Fake email cost a computer company an estimated $2 billion in damage to reputation and lost productivity.
- A European Commission study predicts that junk mail (and spam) is inflicting a cost of about 10 billion euros on business internet users (in wasted time and network resources).
- In a 2001 survey IDC found that 83 per cent of European businesses had a formal email security policy.
- The American Management Association estimated that in 2001 up to 43 per cent of American companies scanned their employees' emails.
- One American airline estimated it cost $312 000 in 'technical effort' alone to recover backup files and restore servers after being hit by the 'I love you' virus. Total worldwide costs were estimated at $8.75 billion.

The good news is that Giga Consulting estimate that anti-spam and content management technology will evolve rapidly over the next 18 months.

> **Counting the corporate cost of personal email**
> If the average hourly salary is S
> In a week it costs you $S \times 5$
> Assuming a 42 hour working week, that is $S \times 5 \times 42 = W$
> Total cost for the organization (of N employees) $= N \times W$

Have you ever stopped to count the cost of personal use of email by employees in your organization? Studies estimate users spend about one hour a week dealing with their own personal non-business related email.

Just taking an average hourly salary of a clerical person at say £13 could be costing you up to £2700 per person, and that does not include the network resources to carry and store such personal emails. If they are downloading large files (say music and video) you could be looking at significantly higher costs both visible and hidden, e.g. slower network response times, need for more storage space, etc. The average three to four minute MP3 music track is around 3 to 5 Mb while a single movie clip in MPEG format would start at around 20 to 30 Mb. Just imagine if you have 100 employees downloading such files during a 12-month period?

Whether you permit personal use of email is only part of the jigsaw. Once you have decided what to do, how do you ensure that employees comply with the policy and best practice guidelines?

By and large the top management team (the board of directors) have inexorably failed to apply their attention and thought to how email should really be used as a vehicle for corporate communications and knowledge sharing. This is not new, as early as 1991 headlines were appearing which read:

> *Regular dose of prevention – Financial Times*, 19 February 1991 – (*... now they* [computer viruses] *are becoming a real problem for businesses ...*)

> *Board's lack of awareness increases IT security risks.*
> *Computer Weekly*, 6 November 1997

Perhaps it has been ignored because tackling these issues will often require a change in behaviour and sometimes culture, and these are things which are hard to achieve. The easy option is to keep doing what we do. But isn't leadership about setting the role model and a good example?

Leaders create futures by emphasizing what the company's people must learn, not by reinforcing what they already know.
Rosabeth Moss Kanter (1992)

We have seen in Parts One and Two how at a personal and team level you can save significant time dealing with your email. However, the dramatic savings come from the board taking charge and engendering a responsible email culture throughout the organization.

In many organizations, email has by default and lack of management changed the way the organization operates. This is particularly true of communications patterns, the way information is shared and the decision-making process. In some cases, as we will see, this has been for the better, but that is often more by luck than chance.

To use any form of technology, from a logistics system to the payroll to gain a business benefit, requires that the people, technology and processes work in harmony as shown in Figure ii (page xvi). Managing the use of email across the organization (no matter how large) is no exception. Once you have a policy and a set of best practice guidelines a major problem is how to control and manage these and ensure that employees comply with them.

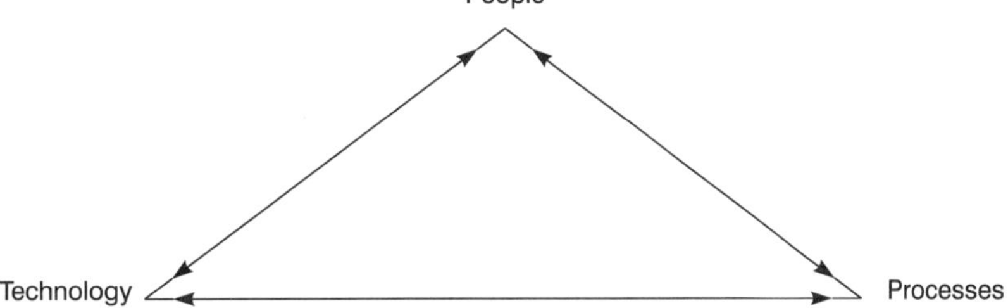

Figure ii
Managing the corporate email

For some organizations it may be sufficient just to have them in place. However, with the rapid increase in spam and the competitive nature of the business world, protecting yourself against virus and spam attacks and managing how content flows in and out of the organization are imperative. To do this requires email management technology too, such as Brightmail, Clearswift ES, MetaSight and SurfControl. All these are software packages capable (to different degrees) of fighting spam and managing content.

This part of the book deals with:

- what your inbox says about your organization in terms of management information cultures;
- how you can use email to support and drive the culture you want rather than let email drive the culture;
- the gender gap – differences in the way men and women use email;
- the impact of email on decision making and how to use email to improve the decision-making process;
- ways to create email best practice behaviour;
- technology to help you manage the content and use of email;
- the email good citizen's charter.

It will provide you with advice and some techniques to try to ensure that email is used more effectively as a corporate management resource and help you save time. The contents are aimed at those already responsible for the corporate use of emails, and those who want to have an impact on the way their organization uses email in the future. An email good citizen's charter is laid out in Chapter 17. (For those needing to write a netiquette style email policy, i.e. the detailed legal requirements, you will need to refer to one of the other published books on this topic such as that by Flynn, 2000.)

The tools and techniques described in this part of the book are appropriate to both large and small organizations and both the public and private sector. They will deliver the same pro-rata return on your investment in time, whether you are a multinational or a sole trader organization. After all, businesses, no matter how large or small, depend for their survival on their brand image and how well they use their assets. This means you and me and the information we communicate internally and externally.

12 Organizational fingerprints in the inbox

Does the culture of the organization influence how we use email?
Does the way we use email change the culture of the organization?
What does the ratio of noise to information say about the organization?

12.1 Introduction

> *Culture and leadership are two sides of the same coin, in that leaders first create cultures when they create groups and organizations. Once cultures exist, they determine the criteria for leadership and thus who will and who will not be a leader.*
>
> Edgar Schein (1992)

Not only is your inbox a fingerprint of how you manage, but it is also a reflection of the broader organizational culture in which you operate. Depending on the size and diversity of your organization as a whole that might be the culture of the whole organization or your subunit, e.g. division, team. No organization ever has just one culture, although in some the overall corporate culture pervades wherever you go. For example, within a public sector organization there is normally one culture, whether you are in either a service or a policy unit. Whereas in a large technology organization there may be multiple cultures depending on whether you are in sales or engineering.

What is meant by culture has been the subject of almost as many papers and books as what we mean by leadership. This is not the place to debate which definition is right or wrong, better or worse, because all have some element of realism. Organizational culture is about the way people behave, the values of the organization, process, the style of management. Within these there are subcultures such as the information and technology cultures.

In the context of email, the way email is used and the organizational culture are two sides of the same coin. The culture will influence the use and the use will influence the culture, especially in respect of the:

- management structure;
- information culture;
- technology culture;
- business process for getting tasks done.

The level of noise and information in your inbox will reflect both your own management style and the culture of your organization. The former is absolutely within your power to control (if you so wish). Your control over the latter will depend on where you stand within the organization and whether you may be able to influence or change it.

In this chapter we review: how the organizational culture can influence the information to noise ratio and what the information to noise ratio says about the organizational culture. Ways to change how email is used at the organizational level are discussed in Chapter 16.

12.2 Words about culture

As indicated, much has been scribed about culture. For the purpose of this book a useful framework, and one which many can relate to, is that of Charles Handy. Handy (1976) posits that there are four main cultures.

Club culture (often also called the power culture) is like a spider's web where the key figure sits at the centre surrounded by ever-widening circles of advisors and intimates. The nearer you are to the centre the greater your influence and power. Typical examples are the way the Prime Minister Mr Blair runs Number 10, family run businesses and start-up companies.

Role culture (often also called bureaucracy) is typified by formal organizational charts and individual logical orderly hierarchical reporting lines. The box in the organizational chart defines what you do and survives long after the occupant moves on. Typical examples are public sector organizations, banks and utilities.

Task culture is best represented as a matrix (or net). People and resources are organized according to projects and can be moved around much more quickly than within a role or even club culture to respond to changing needs. People often have multiple reporting lines. Typical examples are technology companies, consultancies, manufacturers, charities, media companies.

Person culture is the least common as it puts the person rather than the organization first. Resources and people are arranged around a key person so as to draw out their talent. Typical examples are professional organizations such as lawyers, architects, media and doctors.

12.3 The picture of the organization painted by use of email

Go into any organization these days and quite probably somewhere you will see a statement about that organization's values. You know the sort of thing – 'we pride ourselves on offering you excellent service', 'we value your custom'. Directors and managers will often proudly tell us about how their organization functions and how they have changed the culture from being hierarchical to a more open and empowered place to work, with no more 'cover my backside' escapades, and how they value their human and intellectual capital and so on.

Yet, a closer look at people's email inboxes shows them full of cc'd and bcc'd email, one-to-many circular emails, not to mention all the attachments, and much of this is regarded by the recipient as 'not useful'. Having reduced the noise from near neighbours and those they work closely with, when we ask them how they deal with this, the standard reply is 'it comes from head office and I cannot take my name off the global circulation list'.

To illustrate these differences we will use three organizations that we have studied in depth. This is the mean flow of incoming email through the average inbox.

Organization and sector	Average emails received per day	Ratio of noise to information
A – Construction	22	Low information/low noise
B – Government	43	High noise/low information
C – Technology	82	High noise/high information

In organization C it is not unusual for someone to receive up to 150 emails per day. In organization A the maximum was about 40.

12.3.1 Organization A – low information/low noise

Organization A is an international player in the construction industry and has grown from a series of takeovers of smaller like-minded companies. It is an old fashioned paternalistic organization trying to modernize itself. Long service is a signature of this organization. In the UK, the 2200 employees are spread across 250 sites, giving the impression of a flat management structure, and although employees have a certain degree of autonomy there is a strong underlying hierarchical structure.

Major business decisions are made by one of the two senior management committees. This is a classical task culture at the business unit level set within an overarching 'role culture'.

Head office is located in an old building with a mix of traditional offices for the most senior staff and open plan offices for everyone else. It is just merging three main offices and moving to a new purpose-built modern state of the art premises.

12.3.2 Organization A – finance director on the use of email

We are struggling in this business because the common understanding of when to use email is not as far developed. To a certain extent we are misusing/abusing email. We tend to use it for things that we never intended to use it for. It's a medium intended for sharing information. One would hope that one would do short emails that give you bits and pieces of information, arrange meetings or respond quickly to simple questions. When you are getting emails which have 20 attachments and it takes two and a half hours to print it – we are using email outside its initial design. I can read something quicker on a piece of paper than off the screen, especially with columns and numbers.

Initially we had the telephone, then the fax and now we have added email to it. There is a slight culture of email being more of an irritant than of use because people use it for the wrong reasons and therefore it's almost counterproductive.

My approach (like others in the organization) to email is to do it early in the morning, about one hour before the official working day starts.

Now people just drop an email or two rather than making time for face-to-face contact. The problem is that you tend to end up working in a sterile environment. Like an operating theatre, you can see masks not people that say the absolute minimum to each other. I am a firm believer that you have to have regular, one-to-one, eye contact to ensure that they (employees) understand the common objective of the business. It's a way of showing an interest in the individual.

We use email to drive the decision-making process by delivering information through email but it hasn't necessarily speeded up the process. We also use it to delegate authority. People are very focused on their objectives and taking the business forward and will use whatever means. We have a pretty flat structure, which helps.

In this organization email is used but is not necessarily part of the culture. They tend to treat email like internal paper mail, the inbox is read once in the morning and all the email dealt with in one go.

Email was introduced about seven years ago and then only the very senior managers had access to it. The style of emails is still fairly formal. Bad spelling and grammar are not accepted in a play-off against time. Spur of the moment (internal) emails are considered 'to be not thought out' and 'condemned'.

Within the last six months they have launched an email best policy and netiquette policy. Email is currently being used as an efficiency tool to automate processes but not to change and transform the way they do business.

Although they use technology and have a very forward-looking IT department, the company have only recently become entirely dependant on their use of IT to do their business.

In technology terms this organization until recently has been a laggard, it still does not have a global intranet. Although its email system is 'Notes' based it does use the 'Bulletin Boards' function to post some one-to-many type notices and information. Overall the low maturity of use and organizational culture tends towards a low noise and low information profile.

12.3.3 Organization B – high noise/low information

Organization B is a specialist unit within a major government department. It is relatively new, being formed from members of the parent and other government agencies. It develops cross-cutting policies to meet the government's current agenda. It is located in an old listed building and is very cramped and short of space: with coffee areas and corridors doubling for make-shift meeting rooms.

People work on individual projects (usually only one at a time), except 'support staff' and 'researchers' who may provide a service to the whole organization. By and large people work in traditional silos through, as one expects, a traditional vertical hierarchical management structure which ultimately reports to a Minister(s).

There is high staff turnover as people come and go as projects are completed and new ones begin. This is deliberate as you are not expected to work for more than two years in this organization. The small group of core permanent staff all work hard at developing and maintaining an informal, relaxed and friendly atmosphere This is a task culture at the project level within a classical organizational role (bureaucracy) culture.

12.3.4 Organization B – team leader on the use of email

Ours is a very co-operative culture, it's got to be. It's a culture where words are very carefully weighed for nuances because that's how you put messages across. What you don't do around here is have stand-up rows with people but you can do an awful lot by what you say in a message.

Email provides more choice for communication. You can deliberately tailor the style of your email to put across the sort of impression that you want, in a way that you couldn't with a formal minute. So it allows us to be much more subtle about the way we do business. You have to think very hard about who you copy and the way you copy because you might want to send a blind copy or two or three copies of the same thing to different people with different messages.

Email has almost replaced written papers as a form of communication in the sense that we used to write and photocopy papers and now we send them as email attachments. We use it to send all sorts of things from personal notes to key policy papers.

It's integral to everything we do now. It's a good way of gathering information, once you've got a relationship going. You can't send emails to people cold and simply say I want 'x' bit of information because you probably won't get it or you'll get it wrong. You can only really do that with people where you've had personal contact.

In terms of paper conservation and time and energy it's a major improvement. It also gives you much more control over your work as you just see everything that comes in – it's not filtered through a secretary. The use of cc and bcc makes work a lot easier. The Ministers have private email addresses, which we sometimes use, whereas before everything you did was filtered through the private secretary.

We work sufficiently closely with many colleagues that I would expect to send them informal emails even though it's about formal business. The amount of very formal business we do by email is very limited. Face-to-face meetings are still crucial.

When we're clearing a report the responses all come by email but we know what they are as we'd make sure we'd phone around their private offices and weren't going to get any nasty surprises. You might have emails ricocheting backwards and forwards between us and Number Ten, but email is integral to everything we do.

Were the email system to be off for a couple of days then our ability to work would be very seriously impaired because we now depend on

> *it so heavily. Where it's down for three or four hours you can work around it.*
>
> *I check my emails about two or three times a day. I sort of whip through them and deal with them very quickly so I don't waste time. Over the past year we tried an email free day to encourage people to talk more.*

Here email is used as the main form of communication, it has been used to transform how they work. Previously information was sent by paper-based internal mail.

Email is well established and everyone is very comfortable with it. By and large internal emails are casual, although at a very senior level the tone is changed accordingly. Email is used for politics with a small p and reflects to some extent a push information culture where information is pushed out to everyone who might have an interest in it. To some extent this is also damage limitation through a 'cover my backside' operation with lots of cc'd and bcc'd email which pushes up the noise level; email is partly also being used to micro manage and 'hover over people'.

Although there is delegation downwards and a task culture within the unit, overall papers rarely go out without going right up the silo/hierarchy, which is in keeping with a government agency run on traditional role reporting culture.

In terms of maturity of use Organization B is a little more mature than A; they have also made some, albeit very limited attempts, to implement codes of best practice.

12.3.5 Organization C – high noise/high information moving to low noise/high information

Organization C is a leading global technology company, providing computer software, hardware and consultancy. It is in the words of one interviewee 'a company that generally wants to do the right business for its customers. It is a very ethical company; we do the best business with people when we do it for years and years, then we have long-term relationships.' Within service divisions (where our study was based) employees spend a lot of time talking to people (in meetings, on the phone, videoconferencing, etc.). It has a task culture with people having multiple reporting lines.

The organization is passionate about its core values. Its overarching one is 'the passion for business' which emphasizes accountability and working as a team. This is a change from an old culture where individual excellence always counted and was rewarded. Another is to value knowledge and professional expertise. There has also been a move away from decisions based on seniority towards decisions based on knowledge and expertise.

Organization C is in a high tech modern building in a modern industrial complex built within the last decade.

12.3.6 Organization C – head of a business division on the use of email

Like others, I use email all the time, my system is on all day, everyday until I go to bed at the end of the day. You are expected to check your email every half an hour or so. It's our main form of communication. There is a culture in C where you get twitchy unless you replicate your email every few hours. I think millions are sent every day. In Organization C we completely rely on electronic communication.

I don't think we could do business in our company without email. A feature of business today, especially business like ours, which is entirely e-business, is that we have to be able to change our minds. We work in a very volatile and dynamic environment. Email is quite good for that. People send messages that say 'you said you wanted to do this but here's why I think it isn't a very good idea'.

The speed with which we make decisions, the speed with which we run our business, the complexity of the business we are in, none of this would be possible without email. Fourteen years ago when I joined we had email even then, there were patterns of more serial projects being worked on. Now we work on lots and lots of different things at the same time. I don't think we could do that without a sophisticated email system.

Often people work individually: people within a team might not necessarily be on the same site and will not meet face to face for years. Moreover, people don't have to have offices to perform their work from. Email has been a fantastically important tool for them to communicate.

We have different types of electronic communications between people. We have email, now email is becoming a non-simultaneous communications mechanism and it's becoming a one-to-one communication. We might open a dialogue in email regarding a customer account we are both working on and talk about it. However, that's not very helpful or productive for holding a discussion if there's a group of us. We used to have what we call 'team rooms' where we post documents for everyone to comment on or read. Now we are moving to a chat room style environment and 'same time messaging'. Chat rooms are informal communities and are becoming more prevalent. I heard that we have an estimated 85 000 informal communities and 60 formal ones.

It's not something that's been mandated [having informal communities] there's no legislation, no particular dictates. The technology has been made available for people to make a choice and they are beginning to make one.

Same time messaging is like instant messaging: we are both on-line. I might call you and say 'hi are you there' and you come back 'yes' and we start having a conversation about work or an entirely work unrelated one. We might be on a conference call and using same time for an urgent situation to find a solution to a problem.

You have to be careful to differentiate between those who choose to work long hours and did so before email and those who have to. Having to might be to do with not being quite competent in your job or having too much to do. Now the technology just means we have more choices about how we do it and I probably do it more effectively.

People we talk to who only check their email every couple of days have become difficult to deal with because you have an expectation about response which isn't matched.

If the system is down it's like losing your right arm. It's absolutely unbelievable and awful. Recently my hard disk failed, but I wasn't without email for long because in C, it is so important to us that they don't try and mend it [the PC], they just give you a new one and then try and mend it.

Here is an organization at the leading (some might even say 'bleeding') edge of technology. The corporate culture of valuing expertise and knowledge comes through in the communities of interest. The information culture is of pull rather than push. There is a long hours culture and email just makes this easier to work within as much can be done from home. They are very much a task culture at the operational level and one has the impression of a busy organization. People are trusted and there is a very open culture in which opinions can be surfaced for the good of the business rather than personal gains.

Certainly user's inboxes are in the high information side of the noise to information matrix. The question is whether they are high or low noise. In all probability they are on the cusp of the high/low noise intersection. They are mature users of email and have started to explore other ways of using electronic communications. Being able to refine and segment their use of email means they are beginning to be able to reduce the volume of noise and create an even stronger pull information culture. That is, users can go and seek out what they need rather than have it constantly thrown at them.

There is no formal email training as it is assumed that you can use the system. When anyone joins, the organization makes sure you can align the systems to your needs and know what to use when and the capability of each system.

12.4 Comparisons

These case histories show how the content of your inbox can also reflect the wider organizational culture and in particular the:

- ways of working;
- information culture;
- technology culture;
- overall culture in Handy type terms.

In Organization A, email is used as an additional form of communication rather than the principal one in contrast to Organizations B and C, and this reflects the higher volume of email in these two organizations. People rarely take email home in Organization A (except when they are working from home) in contrast to C where home and late at night are often the only time people really get to deal with all the non-urgent email.

Like Organization A, B is still primarily using email for efficiency gains rather than reinventing and transforming how they work, in contrast to Organization C. Although in Organization B email is much more integrated into how they work and their overall work processes.

In each organization there was some form of email best practice and netiquette. The formulation and degree to which it was embodied in the organization varied as you might expect with maturity of use.

One of the reasons why many inboxes are full of noise and especially the one-to-many emails (the to 'all addressee's' in the global address book) is because organizations still see email as the only form of electronic communication. However, as the organization's use of email matures as we saw in Organization C, other ways of communicating electronically are emerging for both one-to-many and even one-to-one, such as chat rooms, personal portals and instant messaging. At the moment though email is being used a bit like an all-purpose hammer to crack all types of nuts. Use of more appropriate and targeted forms of electronic communications would help many organizations reduce the volume of noise in their users' inboxes. Push information cultures typically create lots of noise as we have witnessed in the case histories and especially Organization B. Email enables you to push out information to everyone regardless of whether or not they need or want it. This very much creates a proactive rather than reactive work culture.

No organization has a pure culture and most have subcultures according to the nature of the work being done by that subunit and within there will be various shades of grey. However, these case histories show how the culture of the organization can influence the use of email and vice versa. There is also an element of market sector expectations and influence peeking

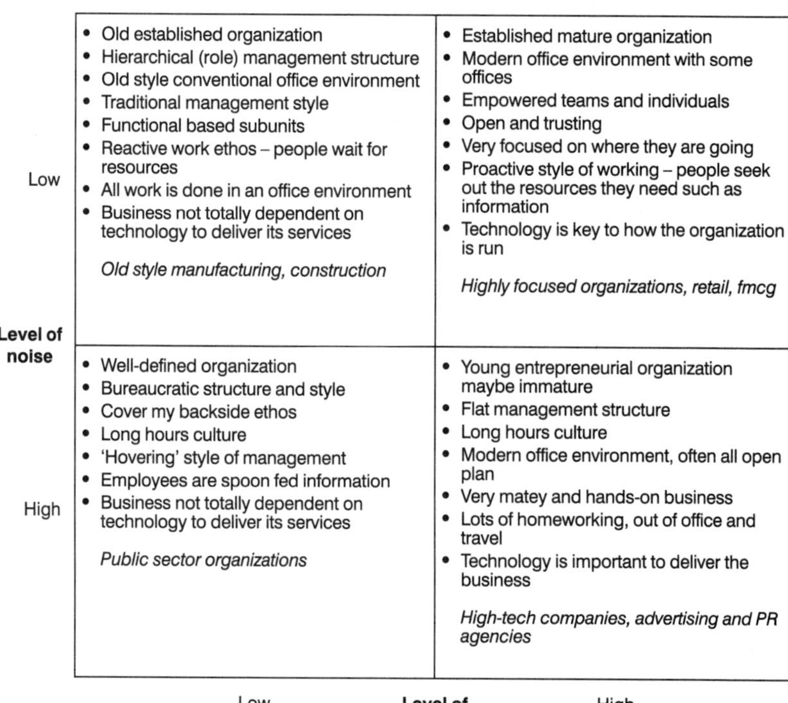

Figure 12.1 Organization cultures and the noise to information matrix

through as you would expect. Porter and Millar (1985) showed that different industries rely to differing extents on information and hence information technology to both produce and deliver their services. Based on this and our own work, Figure 12.1 summarizes typical organizations you might expect to find in the different quadrants of the noise to information matrix.

You might wonder why there is no one case history organization in the low noise/high information quadrant. This of course should be the goal for every organization regardless of size and sector. However, at this point in the history of email, they were hard to find, for the reasons discussed. No doubt, as the top management teams in organizations start to take a more active role in managing how email is used, and learn to differentiate their use of different forms of electronic communication, more will find themselves moving their users towards inboxes which have a low noise and high information content.

12.5 Summary

Just as your inbox says a great deal about how you manage at the individual level so it speaks volumes about your organization's culture. Below are eight questions to ask yourself about what you think your organization's use of email says about your organization (or division) and hence how you could reduce the volume of noise and increase the information content without increasing the overall email traffic. Ways to change corporate email behaviour are discussed in Chapter 16.

1 How much cc'd and bcc'd information was in your inbox last week and what does it say about your organization?
2 How many people log-in either from home outside normal working hours and/or when on leave? What does this say about your organization's culture?
3 What other forms of electronic communication does your organization use?
4 Does your organization send lots of 'all addressee' emails?
5 Does your organization use electronic communications to support other ways of working, e.g. working from home?
6 If your email system went down for more than one hour could your organization continue to operate?
7 Is the way your organization uses email compatible with your organization's espoused values about openness?
8 Does the style of emails in your organization reflect the assumed culture of your organization?

13 The email gender gap

Do men manage their email better than women?
Are women using email more effectively than men?
Who is more likely to be addicted to email, men or women?

13.1 Introduction

Management literature is full of studies about the differences between the way men and women both manage and communicate. Typically such research has revealed differences in style and in particular a tendency for men to be more task focused, more abrupt and less emotional. Women meanwhile are often regarded as possessing better interpersonal skills and being more effective at managing the work–life balance, being more able (often through necessity) to switch off when home and focus solely on the 'life' part of the equation.

Networking has long been regarded as a strong male characteristic with the extreme and ultimate form being the all-male club. Nonetheless, women score when it comes to networking for social outcomes (e.g. finding the babysitter) and providing emotional support.

Given the dominant role email now plays as a communications medium it would not be surprising to see differences emerge in the way men and woman use it. However, perhaps of more interest is the effect email is having, if any, on the difference between the way men and women manage. Is email subversive and broadening the gender gap? Or can we use it to help narrow the gap? Does email play to either the strengths or weaknesses of either gender?

In this chapter we review some of the trends and patterns we have found and how these relate to other studies and the implications for the culture of the organization. You will also find a benchmarking exercise and tips on how to temper your emails if you want the best response from the opposite sex.

13.2 The differences

13.2.1 The email gap

There are eight main differences that we have observed in the way men and women use email and also in their whole attitude towards email:

- Size of the inbox
- Noise to information
- Speed of response
- Tone of the content
- Deletion
- Use and misuse
- Level of email IT fitness
- Desire to stay connected

Size of the inbox and noise to information ratio

For many men and some women, the size of their inbox has become yet another status symbol. The new macho thing to moan (or should we say boast) about is how many emails you receive a day. Never mind the noise to information ratio just look at the total volume is the cry from some. Men in particular compete on volume and if someone is getting a hundred emails a day then the perception is that they must be really important. Although, as others have found they are also prone to exaggerating the size of their inbox (*Britain's First Email Diary* 2001, MSN Hotmail). Consequently, men often have a higher noise to information ratio and tend to be more like Joe – 'the email junkie' or Justin – 'just on line' (see Chapter 2).

Speed of response and tone of content

Email seems to encourage a reckless approach to driving the inbox. There is a tendency for men to respond faster to an email, which is often at the expense of any thought for the recipient. Men tend to be more succinct and very precise particularly when they are writing to women. Men are less inclined to use greetings or to ask social questions about the family or your weekend in an email. Women tend to be more conversational in style, writing longer, more detailed emails. Women are far more likely to take an extra few minutes to compose the content with the recipient in mind. They might even put it in the draft box and mull it over before it's sent:

> *The basis of relationships is connections which means communications. Email can be the bane of our lives but in our frenetic lives it is often the only way. When I send an email, which touches on other people's sensitivities, I spend time composing it. A good manager stays in touch and manages the connections.*
>
> Hilary, marketing director, international telecommunications company

An emerging trend is for senior women to adopt a more terse 'male' style for their emails but this can backfire as it can be perceived as cold or authoritarian coming from a women:

> *Men like to get straight to the point in as few words as possible. They seem less keen on using the phone and find email an easier medium. However, as part of my own email time-management I am now trying to be 'less polite' and more 'male' in my replies. This has significantly reduced the time email takes up.*
>
> Deborah, vice president, international finance organization

Deleting the unwanted email

Men are observed to be better and quicker at deleting unwanted mail. They delete on receipt and regret their haste later. Whereas women tend to hoard messages in their inbox just in case they will be needed.

Men too are far more inclined to delete all their unread emails when they return from leave. Whereas most women will systematically and logically deal with each and every email.

While both sexes randomly cherry-pick the crop of the day's new mail, men are more prone to doing this than women and again will leave the unread mail to atrophy at the bottom of the inbox. In keeping with how they deal with the vacation pile, women are more likely to make sure each and every email has a response.

Use and misuse

There are also some subtle nuances about the way men and women use email. While women are always thought of as gossips, it's men who are more likely to use email to gossip about their love life. For example, the case of Claire Swire who successfully sued her boyfriend for sending an email about their relationship. More recently, a banker from Credit Lyonnais sent an email describing how he performed with his girlfriend to five friends. But they had no time for confidentiality and promptly circulated it to other friends. A chain mail then ensued and in no time the original missive had done the round at several well-respected banking institutions including Barclays, Bank of England, Bloomberg and HSBC, not to mention the *Daily Telegraph* and the Football Association! Needless to say the originator of the email was been suspended from work.

Women on the other hand are far more inclined to use email to catch up with friends and family. Men use email in preference to the phone. They will use email to arrange to socialize sending a curt 'see you in the pub' one liner. Despite the tendency for more men than women to stay connected (and access their email on the move) email is very unlikely to replace the drink in either the pub or wine bar.

Similarly when auditing inboxes it is often the men who send the jokes, although these seem to be appreciated by both sexes as underpinned by this comment from a colleague: 'I always read all my messages when I come back from leave otherwise I might miss a good joke' (Julie, a conference organizer). When it comes to politics, men are more inclined to use email.

Level of email IT fitness and desire to stay connected

Men generally have a higher level of IT fitness. All the gold users we know are men, but by the same token most of our bronze users are also men! As indicated men are more inclined to want to stay connected and try out all the latest gizmos to do so. That is not to say that women do not also access their emails on the move – indeed many do so. It is just that men are more likely to choose to stay connected. Perhaps unsurprisingly, most executive women are silver or high bronze users

Summary

These variations are based on our observations of over 175 men and women with whom we have worked and specific research into gender differences and the use of email by Mesmo Consultancy.

Nonetheless, other studies have found similar differences (such as Mallon and Oppenheim 2002 and Panteli 2002). Research by MSN Hotmail found that men are more likely to flirt by email than women. Indeed, edesign.co.uk found that while 30 per cent of men will use email to flirt only 15 per cent of women will flirt by email. Conversely edesign.co.uk found that over 30 per cent of women use email at work to plan their social life. So you could argue that to some extent both sexes are guilty of abusing the office email system!

It is well known that in general men are more likely to log onto the internet than women (Russell and Drew 2001 and Russell and Stafford 2002). Indeed the 2002 survey revealed that men spend about 30 per cent more time on the internet than women (8.3 hours per week compared to 5.3 hours for females). However, all is most likely to change with the push to make technology and especially IT more appealing to women. Or will it? Are there some lessons we can learn about how to save ourselves time and use email to communicate more effectively?

13.3 What does this tell us?

Some of the more widely accepted differences between the way men and women manage are summarized in Table 13.1. (This is based on a review of the recent literature by Vinkenburg *et al.* 2000.)

Clearly, such differences, if that is even the right word, are often moderated by circumstances such as the organizational culture and context. Indeed as Vinkenburg *et al.* suggest, 'continuity' might be a better description. While this is not the place to argue the true extent of these variations, it does provide a framework from which to review the differences in how men and women use email and the possible explanations.

By and large the differences in attitudes to, and use of, email is mainly a reflection of these underlying behavioural attributes.

Table 13.1 Gender differences in management styles and behaviour

Women – the likelihood	Attribute/Characteristic	Men – the likelihood
Less	Risk taking	More
More	Relationship focused	Less
More	Communal	Less
More	Interpersonal	Less
More	Supportive	Less
Less	Image conscious	More
Less	Autocratic	More
More	Participative	Less
Less	Directive	More
Less	Self-confident	More
Less	Career networking	More
More	Social networking	Less
More	Emotional support networking	Less
Less	Political	More

For example, the desire to stay connected reflects the fact that women are far better at making the work–life equation balance – often through necessity. When they are home they are more likely to be able to switch off and focus all their attention to the home front.

The trend towards a higher level of IT fitness among men reflects several interrelated factors. First, the underlying trend for technology to appeal more to men than women. Second, the propensity for men to be more status conscious and wanting always to have the latest 'toys for the boys'. The need to have overt status symbols also accounts in part for the new trend towards perceiving the size of the inbox as directly proportional to importance and hence a trend towards a greater noise to information ratio.

Women are generally regarded as possessing greater interpersonal skills and higher emotional intelligence and this is clearly reflected in the style of their emails. Women have a tendency to feel less self-confident and this too is echoed in the more detailed self-justifying content rather than using a confident one line response.

The short terse male type emails probably also reflect poor keyboard skills, as typing can be perceived as a 'woman's skill or work'. Men have been brainwashed into thinking that touch typing is for girls and many are reluctant to use more than one hand let alone all the fingers. But this is changing, as an increasing number of male executives are now actively developing their keyboard skills and learning to touch type! A recent survey of what was on 25 top executives New Year's wish lists revealed that for at least 25 per cent being a faster typist was one item. In addition, many business courses now include learning touch typing as a training module.

Again following the stereotype, men tend to be inherently lazier than women. This encourages shorter messages, abbreviations and the quicker scanning and deletion approach. While this may save time for the sender it is not without its downsides:

> *Men abbreviate in emails too much and, being skim-readers, may fail to read to the end of their messages. Which means that you are forced to add to the email mountain by sending the whole thing again.*
>
> Ruth Bishop, human resources director, Securitas, in 'Men shoot from the hip. Women agonise'. Virginia Matthews, *The Guardian*, 12 August 2002

Politicking has always been synonymous with corporate life and climbing the greasy pole of the corporate hierarchy. As one might expect, men are also more inclined to use email for politics.

Lastly, email as a networking tool. Women have long since valued networking for providing social and emotional support, but only recently have joined the career networking party. It is therefore not surprising that women use email for keeping in touch with friends and family. Again there is also an element of the life side of the work–life balance creeping in here.

13.4 How macho are you about email?

How macho are you when it comes to email? Are your emails from Mars or Venus?

13.4.1 The macho email index – a self-assessment exercise

Look at the statements below, and circle the number you feel most accurately equates to how you handle your inbox.

1	I prefer just to get across the point and not worry about style and grammar, etc.	1	2	3	4	5	I take time to make sure my emails are well constructed and are clearly presented
2	I frequently use text message style shorthand, e.g. Tx for thanks	1	2	3	4	5	I rarely use text message style shorthand
3	Once I've written an email I always send it	1	2	3	4	5	Sometimes I write an email but after reflection either do not send it or modify the contents
4	I nearly always start and sign off my emails in the same way, regardless of who is the recipient	1	2	3	4	5	I usually adjust the salutation and sign off according to the person to whom I am writing
5	Mostly, I scan my inbox very quickly and just read the ones I think are important	1	2	3	4	5	I try to read all my emails systematically even if I don't think they are important to me
6	I am very good at deleting emails which I feel I do not require	1	2	3	4	5	I tend to keep the majority of my emails, just in case
7	There are quite a lot of unread emails in my inbox	1	2	3	4	5	There are almost no unread emails in my inbox
8	When I return to the office after being absent (on work or leave) I often just delete the whole inbox without reading it	1	2	3	4	5	No matter how many emails there are when I have been away from the office, I try to deal with all of them
9	Email is the default communications medium for me, I rarely use any other medium (e.g. phone)	1	2	3	4	5	Although I use email, I try to use other ways of communicating my message whenever possible (e.g. phone)
10	I often talk about how many emails I receive and send	1	2	3	4	5	I rarely talk about how many emails I receive and send

Total your score for the boxes you have ticked and enter your score below.

10		20		30		40	50

Emails from Mars **Adaptable** **Emails from Venus**

13.4.2 Interpreting your score

10–19 The Mars approach Very macho. You might be quick at handling your inbox, but be missing important information by not being a little more empathetic towards your recipient and the needs of others

20–29 A macho air You still exude an air of arrogance in the way you handle your email. Maybe it is just the pace of life which stops you being more thoughtful and tuned into the needs of others

30–39 Androgynous You are able to balance your own needs to those with whom you work and play to the strengths and weaknesses of both sexes

40–50 The Venus approach You may be erring too far on the side of female caution and emotional intelligence at the expense of your personal time constraints and the demands of your own job. You might be too thoughtful for your own good

13.5 How can we work together even better?

To some extent email works against many of the female values which we all value within our organizations. Left to its own, email is in danger of widening the gap between the sexes and alienating women even further. If women feel they really should make their emails more macho then this will just reinforce the male culture, which dominates many organizations. Email is already a thin communications medium devoid of any emotions. We can learn from the Venus approach to email to add a little feeling without being too chatty and effusive.

Conversely, email knows no organizational or hierarchical boundaries. As such if offers women an unparalleled opportunity to have their say and network with the boys.

13.6 Summary

Here are five tips on how to adapt your style of dealing with email to bridge the gender gap, to play to the other person's strengths and the many opportunities offered by email.

For men	For women
Add some feelings	Shorten your emails
Use less text messaging shorthand	Hit the delete key more often
Think before you hit the send key	Worry less about the recipient and more about the task in hand
Use a variety of salutations and sign-offs	Use a variety of salutations and sign-offs
Stop gossiping on-line about your love life	Start using email for career networking

14 Decision making in the email office

How does your organization make decisions?
Do you use email as part of the decision-making process?
Does the use of email improve decision making in your organization?

14.1 Introduction

Email is now an integral part of all aspects of organizational life and has become essential for day-to-day functioning. In general, the use of email seems to facilitate decision making in many positive ways. However, its use in the decision-making process presents many challenges and needs careful management.

The main benefit of using email in decision making is that it allows communication to be made more easily and quickly between colleagues wherever they are in the global business world. In addition, it enables us to send large amounts of supporting information to aid a particular decision that otherwise would have had to be sent by courier or fax taking hours or days rather than seconds. With email you can send as much information as needed, simply by sending files or jpegs (pictures or diagrams) as attachments. This effectively compresses the data and because of the speed of transferring data, the size of the file does not become a major factor in the impediment of its transmission. (Although, transmission of large data files can be slowed by modem speed, network availability, etc.)

Email has become a very important addition to the choices we have of how and when we communicate during and following the decision-making process. (For example, we must decide when it is appropriate to use a personal phone call, a teleconference, personal or group email, intranet notice, face-to-face personal or group meeting and so on.) Good communication is essential when making a decision. It enables you to gather the information you need and will also allow you to tell people about the decision that has been made in a timely, effective and appropriate manner. This ensures that the decision can be acted on as soon as possible. Email is now an intrinsic part of the whole process in most organizations. In particular, it allows more people's opinions to be taken into account regarding the points of the decision. This means a more informed and possibly fairer decision can be made with potentially less risk.

14.2 Corporate decision making

Herbert A. Simon (US Social Scientist) defines a decision as:

> *A moment in an ongoing process of evaluating alternatives for meeting an objective at which expectations about a particular course of action impel the decision maker to select the course of action most likely to result in attaining the objective.*

In some organizations the decision-making process is very formal. This may include:

- Formal diagnostic processes
- Feasibility studies
- Consultation processes
- Committee meetings
- Trials and testing of options

For some, decision making is far less formal and may simply be reactive considerations to ongoing operational issues. Whatever the process successful organizations 'outdecide' their competition in at least three different ways:

- They make faster decisions
- They make better decisions
- They implement decisions more regularly

In addition, they almost certainly use email as an integral part of their decision-making process.

When assessing the impact that emails have had on decisions, a simple model is needed to represent the decision-making process. Several common characteristics emerge from the many models developed over the years.

The model shown in Figure 14.1 recognizes six stages from which all decisions are made. Email can play a part in all six stages. The gathering of information (i.e. the determination and evaluation of options and understanding the problem) is greatly affected by email. Specifically, email enables more information

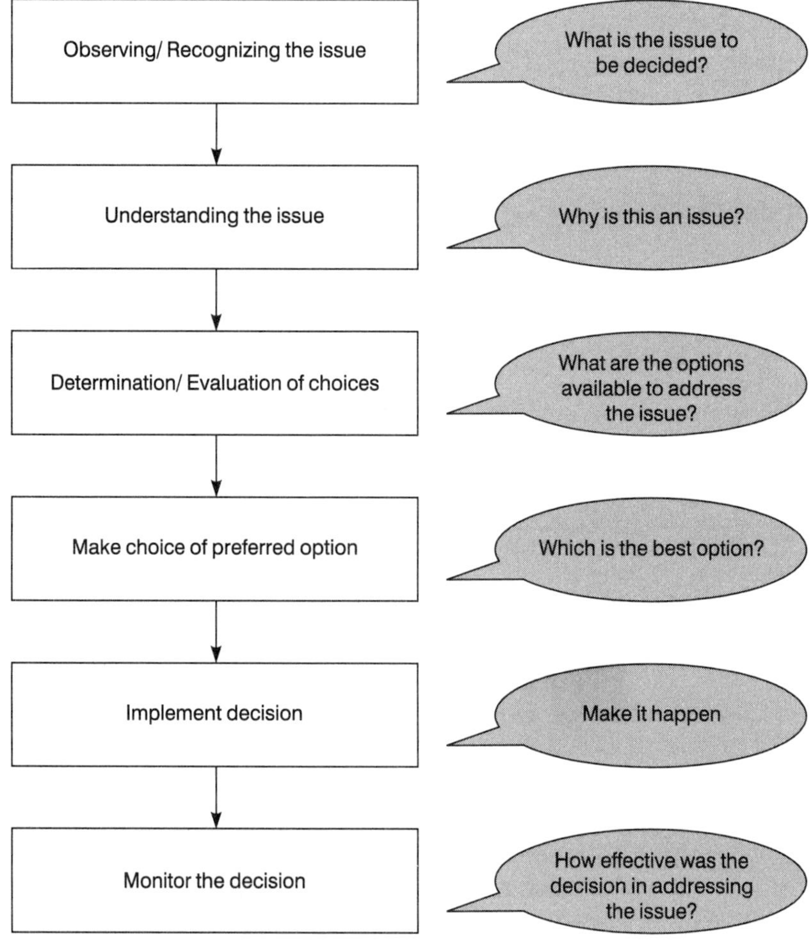

Figure 14.1 Six stage decision-making model.

to be exchanged quicker and more easily between parties and decisions communicated much more speedily.

As in other areas of business, email can also have a negative impact. In decision making this can be due to the fact that people can abuse email by copying too many people onto an email – resulting in people receiving irrelevant emails or emails that they do not need to receive. This can slow down the whole process.

14.3 The impact of email on decision making

Having identified the decision-making process and where email can play a part it is worth looking at the impact that email has had on organizations and decision making.

For routine decisions the effect of email has been to increase efficiency without any loss in effectiveness.

Many of the decisions that we have to take each day are made using email. They require only a brief yes or no response and email has made this process quicker. Using email as opposed to another communication method takes less time and an immediate response can be gained.

Any increase in efficiency will of course be dependent on the situation and the nature of the decision to be made. Arranging diary dates by email can be far more time consuming than a simple phone call. This is especially true if it only involves one other person. Saying 'yes' to a request is easy by email but if it is 'no' it may be more polite to make a phone call or visit the person if they are nearby. In this case email would have no effect.

Generally it seems that for very simple routine decisions where there are no concerns about form and content, email has increased efficiency, but there are still some routine decisions where email is not the appropriate communication method.

Using email in the decision-making process will lead to a greater availability of information.

This in turn will lead to increased effectiveness where adaptive and innovative solutions are required. The greater availability of information can be both an actual increase in the volume of relevant information received and also an increase in the accessibility of those people who take part in the decision making. Like many aspects regarding the increased use of email, this can be both positive and negative. Using email as part of decision making is likely to cause more information to be circulated and this in turn can lead to more meetings. Also more information does not necessarily mean better information. Much of the additional information we receive now is as a result of being included in various emailing lists and news wires. As we discussed in Chapter 8 much of this unnecessary information used to be filtered out by secretaries and PAs when it was in paper form. As inboxes are now generally managed personally this has led to a decrease in the amount of secretarial filtering of information.

The efficiency of email as a communication method in decision making is reduced when recipients receive a large volume of irrelevant information. It is estimated that around 10–25 per cent of email received on a regular basis is irrelevant. Clearly this can create information overload and slow down the decision making.

14.3.1 Increased accessibility of senior management

In addition to the sheer volume of emails received, senior management has become more accessible by the use of email. Email has removed many hierarchical barriers and made it easier to respond to the most pressing issue first regardless of who sent it. Email allows people outside of the work group to provide input to a decision process and also allows more people to be better informed during the process.

Email appears to be less effective for decisions of a more personal or emotional nature. This is because vital information such as the tone of voice, gestures and other communication tools are lost, which can often lead to misunderstandings.

14.3.2 The use of email can speed up decision making

While this is undoubtedly true, the downside to the almost instant communication of email is that some decisions are being made too hastily without due consideration of all the facts and options. When using email, people expect things to be done straight away which often results in rushed decisions.

14.3.3 Email can allow decisions to be communicated more easily

A decision has not been made until it has been communicated to the relevant people and email can be the most speedy and effective way of doing this. Before email, communication was either by phone or often in a more formal written format. Email is a graduation between the two and so can be easily tailored to put across the right impression. If email is used in the first place to arrive at the decision, it follows that the final decision should be communicated by electronic means. Email can be the best way to communicate decisions of a time-sensitive or complex nature. For example, when it is important to say exactly the same thing to all people at the same time. In the electronic office, email is the best way to communicate decisions, as paper documents are increasingly less likely to be read.

While this is true for most decision making, it is perhaps less so when dealing with subjects of a more personal or sensitive nature. Email would not be the most appropriate form of communication to inform successful or unsuccessful job applicants of your decision. It is not a personal enough method and in situations like this a paper letter can be better for record-keeping purposes. However, this is changing and many companies now strive to be more 'paperless' and have a policy of keeping e-records in line with much that is happening in the field of e-government. However, if your company does not have an e-policy of this nature it is still safer to print off decisions or records received by email and file them manually as you would have done in the past. (It goes without saying that you should back up onto CD or floppy disk all your email and PC data regularly, in case you lose all your electronic records.)

Decisions can be made more easily and therefore be better monitored as a result of using email.

Once a decision is in the implementation phase the use of email as part of the monitoring process enables problems to be dealt with before they escalate and do significant damage. Email provides managers with a speedy and effective way of staying informed of their current projects. This is particularly the case when managing remote teams or when the manager is out of the office for considerable amounts of time.

14.4 Summary

Emails will never completely replace face-to-face contact in decision making.

Emails are of enormous help in making, communicating, implementing and monitoring decisions, but sometimes it is better to actually meet or talk on the telephone with the people concerned. The inbox analysis in the previous chapter revealed that many emails are concerned with arranging or following up meetings and telephone calls. Many of the people we spoke with said that they would often follow up an email with a phone call in order to generate a discussion or to check the email had been received and understood. Therefore, face-to-face contact is still necessary when decisions are being made. Additionally email cannot easily be used for anything requiring a group debate. If a number of people are involved in the decision it is often better to meet at the beginning. This helps build relationships, which can be of value further down the line especially if difficulties arise.

When it comes to decision making the most successful people are the ones who know what they don't know and will go to the right people to help them make the right decision. Email can speed up this process and allow more people to be involved.

15

Technology to manage corporate email traffic

How can technology help my organization manage the flow of emails?
What are the issues associated with email management software?
What are the benefits of using email management software?

15.1 Introduction

Once you have defined your email policy (netiquette) and charter for best practice, there is still the question of how to ensure that users comply with the policy. For many a sound training and development programme may be sufficient. In other cases more support is needed in terms of how the content of emails is managed. How do you really ensure that defamatory emails are not circulated internally or externally, that confidential information is not leaked, and so on? Similarly, how can you help employees counter the increasing number of unsolicited junk mail (spam) and virus attacks?

This is where anti-spam, anti-virus and content management software can be invaluable. Better content management is not just about limiting the risks. It can be a business enabler creating opportunities to work smarter and be more responsive to customers.

It is also important to understand that email security is not just about not letting in or out emails and content which might harm the organization. You may need to email highly confidential information. How can you ensure that only the person it is intended for sees the email? How can you be sure that no one tampers with the content of an email? How can you reassure external partners that your systems are secure?

There are a number of levels and ways in which technology can help you control what information goes in and out through email and how to secure that information while in transit. This chapter contains a brief overview of the different types of email management software and systems, the issues associated with formally controlling how email is used, and the benefits to be obtained from using email management software.

15.2 Email management technology

This area of email management is still in its infancy and as such it is hard to draw clear-cut definitions and position the various players in particular markets. In essence there are four broad types of technology:

- Anti-virus software to combat virus attacks such as the 'I love you', Melissa and Bugbear.
- Anti-spam software – designed to block unwanted attacks from outside.
- Filtering software (or content management software as it is sometimes called) – which manages the flow of emails internally and outside the organization in terms of both inbound and outbound email.
- Security systems to transmit email securely (e.g. encryption systems).

There are a number of suppliers as shown by the data in Figure 15.1. The merits of each company cannot be debated in this chapter. Rather, the purpose of this chapter is to create awareness of the potential solutions and opportunities created by such software systems.

15.2.1 Anti-virus software

This is the most established of the management tools and it would be fair to say that most IT departments have imple-

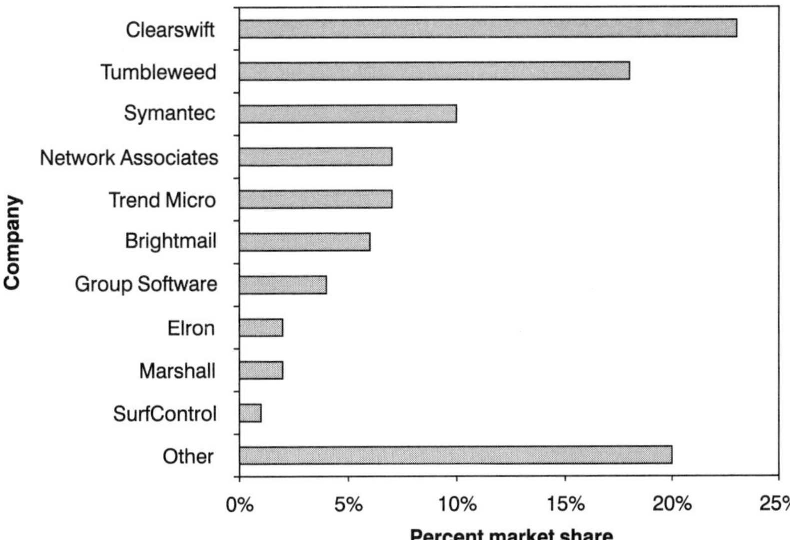

Figure 15.1 Global email content security market (Source: IDC, July 2002)

mented some form of anti-virus software. Plenty of well-established software and systems exist for both corporate and individual users. The only point worth reiterating is the need for those who work on their own (as self-employed or sole traders) to make sure you keep up to date with all the latest updates.

Yes, it's boring and maybe feels a bit geeky to be updating your anti-virus software. However, viruses do not acknowledge any organizational boundaries: they make no distinction between how you are employed or what your position is in the organization! We know of several colleagues who have been attacked by some of the recent viruses such as Bugbear. Always be vigilant about not opening unexpected or unusual attachments and fastidious about updating your software.

15.2.2 Anti-spam software

This will filter email based on key words in order to prevent unwanted email from entering the organization and particularly in the form of unsolicited junk mail or 'spam' as it is so often called.

It is not quite clear why junk mail is called spam. The two theories are that it is named after the ubiquitous canned meat of the same name, which is spiced ham (and was first produced in 1937 by Homel Food Corp.). The other related theory is that the term spam is based on the Monty Python sketch about a restaurant where spam (the meat) was served with everything regardless of whether or not you ordered it.

As such, spam is the unsolicited junk mail, rather than the stuff that comes to you as result of an interaction between you and the sender, e.g. you attended a conference and now receive emails of no interest to you – junk mail. Incoming email can be intercepted based on a number of criteria such as email address types, phrases, type of attachments, and number of people in the address line. Some examples are show below.

Criteria	**Example**
Subject line words and phrases	Sex, Viagra, relaxation Nothing to lose Make money fast Lose weight Save a friend
Email address type	From designated providers such as Hotmail and Yahoo, one with specific formats and especially numerals, e.g. 135Jan@hotmail.com
Attachment types	MPEG, exe

This is the absolute minimum level of filtering software you should have in place. Increasingly organizations are implementing some form of anti-spamming software, either on their own server or as part of the ISP services they purchase. Typical players in this part of the market include Brightmail, Clearswift, Tumbleweed and SurfControl. These companies will have a proprietary list of known 'spammers' that they regularly update and use to round up and trap the usual suspects. Savings made by anti-spam software will depend on the volume you receive and typically range from 5 to 20 minutes per employee per day!

Such software is not cheap and is generally designed for 'enterprise' use (by corporates). For the self-employed, there are a number of less expensive software packages and services designed for the small office and home user such as SpamKiller from McAfee and Spamex from Spamex. The former works on the filtering basis, while Spamex hides your real email address and creates a 'disposable one'.

But what about protecting the emails that leave your organization and contain either potentially harmful information such as confidential data or data that could be regarded as libellous, e.g. about a person or client? Also how do you control the flow of sensitive information within the organization, e.g. who has access to personnel data, sales forecasts, etc.?

15.2.3 Filtering (content management) software

The next level up is the ability to control the content of emails that flow across both the internal and external boundaries of your organization. Filtering software (content management software) is based on the same principles as anti-spam software. Emails both for internal and external purposes are scanned for key words and stopped before they either leave the organization or in the case of internal use reach an inappropriate person.

The ability to scan outgoing email and the degree of accuracy (number of false positives) is primarily what distinguishes the key providers. For example, the more advanced solutions allow you to filter at many different levels of granularity, for example individually by person, by group, by division or by the organization as a whole. Similarly there is some way and degree of sophistication by which the content is filtered. At the crudest level it is on word association alone, for example all emails with the words salary and grade are not allowed to be sent to users outside the personnel department.

At a more advanced level some software works on word association and context, so the words salary and grade when separated by say six words can be let through the filter. SurfControl use adaptive reasoning and artificial intelligence to train the software. It reads documents in order to build up a list of sensitive words that can then be used to filter emails.

At the highest and most sophisticated end of content management is the ability to manage automatically incoming email. For example, emails requesting help or information can be redirected at source rather than left sitting in someone's inbox until they can deal with it. This is moving into the realms of e-marketing. In this respect, content management can enable you to work more smartly with your clients, prospects and even partners, and thus create new business opportunities.

15.2.4 Filtering software with a training component

One unusual and somewhat unique product (currently) is MetaSight from Morphix. This enables an organization not only to monitor breaches in the email policy, but to also make a 'training intervention'. Suppose using 'Reply All' is considered an unacceptable email behaviour and you want to stop this. MetaSight will monitor who is using 'Reply All' and then send a message about how they should behave. The change in behaviour after such an intervention can be quite dramatic as shown in Figure 15.2.

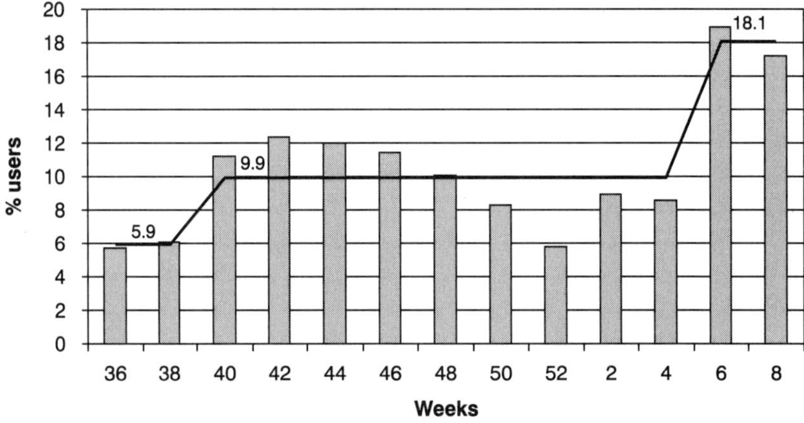

Figure 15.2 Changes in user's behaviour after training. (Source: MetaSight. © 2002 The Morphix Company Ltd. Used with permission)

One aspect of behaviour 'use of subject line prefixes' to comply with company standards was tracked across part of an organization with 2000 users. The first intervention (a personalized message with feedback statistics and education) was made in early October (week 40) and the per cent of good users increased. After the initial increase and as bad practice crept back in, a second reinforcement intervention was sent in early February the next year (week 6). A much larger change was now observed. 'We are after all dealing with people who forget, and a greater change effect can be achieved in the reinforcement intervention, and indeed interventions become more effective over time', commented Mark Newman, Managing Director of Morphix.

MetaSight affords a neat way to tie in codes of best practice with content management designed to improve productivity.

15.2.5 Security systems

Most email policies caution against sending sensitive and confidential information by email and especially over the internet, e.g. personnel data, marketing plans, new business strategies and product specifications. However, many is the time that you will need to transmit such data by email. The concerns then are:

- privacy – the email is only seen by the intended recipient;
- data integrity – has anyone tampered with the content (and attachments);
- authenticity – how does the recipient know the email is from the named sender;
- proof of receipt – how does the sender know the recipient has received the email.

For this you need to use some form of email security technology such as encryption software. This is a relatively mature, albeit underused, form of email management. However, there are several good sources of information on the available options (for example, the National Computer Centre). The main reason for underutilization is that few directors realize how much valuable information seeps out of their organization every day and leaves the organization open to potentially damaging risks.

15.3 Issues

These types of software make extra demands on the processing power needed to run your email system. The other major issue that needs consideration relates to intrusion into people's privacy. Checking the content and patrolling how people use email can be regarded as an intrusion of privacy. Employees are entitled to be protected by the Data Protection Act and this has to be balanced against the need to operate the business. More often than not legislation has favoured the employee.

This is a complex and controversial area as witnessed by the recent furore over the Regulation of Investigatory Powers (RIP) Act. You should seek specialist legal advice. At the very least, you must make it clear to employees what you are doing, and why, and gain their consent. This can be through a clause in their contract and screen that comes up each time they log-in. That said, by and large employees take a positive attitude and are thankful to have at least some of the spam removed.

The key to successfully introducing such software lies in educating users about what and why you are doing it and further underlines the need for a proper email netiquette policy:

> *You have to communicate what is acceptable to employees, so that they can manage themselves. If you do tell them filtering is in place and explain what it means, most people don't mind.*
>
> Steve Purdam, chief executive of SurfControl

This is a contentious matter, and the current issues associated with the legal, regulatory and compliance aspects are well covered in other books (e.g. Flynn, 2000). Many of the national newspapers carry regular commentaries on email monitoring, not least as the EU laws change.

15.4 Benefits

The benefits to be gained from using technology to manage the flow of emails inbound and outbound will obviously depend on the problems you are trying to solve and the opportunities you want to create.

Misuse of email and any consequential staff dismissal carries high costs. These include not just the visible ones of legal and dismissal proceedings but also replacement costs, damages to staff morale and customers' perceptions. A recent survey by Websense found that over 72 per cent of companies have had to deal with internet misuse. Steve Purdam of SurfControl believes that 'disciplinary cases of Internet and email abuse now outnumber dishonesty, violence and health and safety issues put together'. In many cases talking to the offender can solve the problem. Nonetheless, anything that can limit the risk and damage liability must surely be seen as helpful, even if it requires delicate handling.

Some of the benefits that users have realized include:

- improved productivity, i.e. by reducing time spent on non-work related email activities;
- increased available bandwidth;
- reduced risk of litigation;
- protection of company assets in the form of sensitive and confidential information;
- enhanced customer relationships by improving processes for handling incoming customer enquiries;

- better network resource planning;
- enhanced employee relationships.

15.4.1 Case history – Standard Life

Standard Life Assurance Company is Europe's largest mutual life assuror and is only one of six life assurance groups to have a Triple 'A' rating from Standard & Poor's and Moody's the international ratings agencies. The company operates internationally with offices in Europe, Canada, India, China and Bermuda. Current daily volume of email is 40 000 with 25 000 internal and 15 000 external.

Bob Cunningham, senior project manager in IS Operational Services at Standard Life's Edinburgh head office:

> *We had been well aware of the opportunities and risks posed by email throughout the enterprise for sometime and were also keen to protect our employees from spam and abusive email from outside. Some of the costs associated with failing to manage that risk are: legal costs, replacement of staff, productivity losses, the time and effort to recover systems [that have crashed through overload] and reduced storage availability.*
>
> *There is a legal responsibility to protect our employees from that type of abuse and we are very active in this area. We are not here to be big brother and catch people out. It is a case of covering all our options. If you are not seen to take enough action you are liable for legal action.*
>
> *We have a group who identify all the risks which comprises representatives from Human Resources and our Information Protection department. They are my customers.*
>
> *In 2001 they identified that a system was needed to monitor email, to alert us to breaches in the company email policy and also to comply with employee legislation.*

Standard Life implemented Clearswift's ES ClearEdge content management software. In addition to significantly reducing the spam and associated risk, for which they planned, there have been some other unplanned benefits:

> *We are now able to very accurately plan and predict machine requirements such as storage and bandwidth. Before it was a little 'touchy-feely', think of a number and double it. Now we are calculating a potential 30 per cent saving over previous estimates.*

Also, we believe in developing our staff, it's part of our culture. That means giving them the right tools at the right time and making sure they are used appropriately through training. Our employees represent the company and we must ensure they communicate appropriately. This [ES ClearEdge] is not a major tool but it is an important one – it helps make sure that messages going out are professional.

What advice does Bob offer to others embarking on this route?

You must have the policy in place first, and then ask yourself what is the risk and what is at risk if the policy is breached. Tools like this can only complement the policy and best practice guidelines. As circumstances change you may need to revisit the policy and how you use the software.

15.5 Is your organization at risk?

Do you know if your organization has the facility to manage the flow of inbound and outbound emails? Here is a checklist of questions to help you think about what might be appropriate.

15.5.1 Email content risk checklist

1. Has your organization been the victim of a malicious attack from either spam or a virus?
2. Has your organization been involved in any form of legal action through misuse of email?
3. When was the last time anyone assessed the risks from email abuse of any sort (from circulating offensive emails internally to transmitting confidential information outside the organization)?
4. Does your organization have an explicit email policy and code of best practice?
5. When did you last read anything about your company's email policy and best practice?
6. When was the last time you received any training about the email policy and code of best practice?
7. Who owns the policy and code of best practice?
8. Does your company have the ability to manage email content that is consistent with the policy?
9. To what level and in what depth can your organization generate email usage reports (e.g. by person, by type, by department, etc.)?

10 How flexible is that software to meet different individual users' and groups of users' needs?

15.6 Summary

With the volume of spam predicted to increase by up to 23 per cent, the need to filter incoming email, as a minimum, will become increasingly pressing. At present such abuse is still mainly confined to the desktop environment and has yet to reach the mobile phone environment. However, with the implementation of 3G phones capable of downloading content spamming the mobile user cannot be far away. The need to protect corporate data assets is much more important with the increase in mobile computing and users accessing emails on the move. Whatever policy and code of best practice you decide to implement, the technology is now available to support you. Although not yet widely utilized, especially content management, this will change dramatically in the next year or so.

As Paul Rutherford, chief marketing officer at Clearswift, says, to use email effectively to communicate and manage information you must *establish* the policy, *educate* the users and *enforce* your policy. The next chapter is about the process of establishing the policy, best practice behaviour and educating the users. This chapter provided an overview of the technology available to help you and your organization enforce the policy and code of best practice.

16 Ways of creating email best practice

How easy is it to change the way people use email?
Is there a recipe to follow that will guarantee success?
What have other organizations achieved?

16.1 Introduction

Real strategic change requires not merely re-arranging the established categories, but inventing new ones.

Mintzberg (1994)

Suppose you decide you want to change the overall behaviour of the organization. Maybe you want to become more customer focused or to improve the quality of the goods and services your company provides. How would you start to plan for, and subsequently manage, such a change? Of course, you would identify the problems, crystallize the exact behaviour you wanted to develop, set goals, identify the best methodology to achieve these outcomes, involve top management, provide a training programme, and so on. Our point is that this is a long-term process that requires sustained effort.

All change, no matter how small or large, requires us to work at adopting the desired new behaviour. Think about some of the changes you have experienced, from large to small, and insignificant to significant. For example, one of those life-wrenching experiences such as moving house, divorce or the death of a loved one to the more mundane but still unsettling experiences of moving offices or even desks. If you were to plot how you felt, you would find that you experienced the same emotional ups and downs, although the intensity and duration of these peaks and troughs would vary according to trauma of the event.

So why should changing the way we use email be any different? Although, we all have complex personalities, each of us also has some dominant traits, which have become our signature behaviour and this is reflected in the way we use email. They can lead us to act like 'Pat – the pen', 'Joe – the email junkie', 'Justin – just on-line' and or 'Ronnie – the reliable email citizen' (see Chapter 2).

Most organizations have an email policy that relates to the more mechanistic and formal aspects of using email, some of which represent a potentially dismissible offence, such as circulating pornographic material. Such formal policies are often called 'netiquette'. However, far, far fewer organizations have any guidelines akin to a best practice charter, which embodies some form of values about how we should behave and manage our email or even how this links to the corporate values and brand image of the company. In the absence of any such team or corporate behavioural guidance, depending on our email personality, most of us have developed some deeply ingrained habits such as defaulting to email when a face-to-face meeting or phone call might be better.

And now someone (or 'they') have decided we should use email differently? For example, you may have been faced with an instruction that your data storage limit was being reduced, meaning you must delete or archive material otherwise it will all be deleted. This will be to save the company significant storage costs and it might reduce the need to increase the size of its server(s) and lessen other IT costs. All of these areas can impact seriously on the company's profitability and most probably whether or not you will get a bonus. This is why you should bother. If everyone in the company reduced the size of their inbox and freed up some space on the server it could have a very positive effect on the bottom line, your pocket and your productivity.

There are a number of activities you can adopt to support your email best practice campaign such as email-free days and good housekeeping events. However, underpinning these is a need for a properly planned change management programme that is supported from the top and which clearly demonstrates 'what's in it' for everyone at every level of the organization.

Managing enduring change does not happen overnight and just launching a set of email best practice guidelines or having an email-free Friday is no guarantee that either anyone will buy into the change or that it will be enduring. It might make a transient difference for a day or so but after that it will be back to play as usual.

This chapter contains:

- the email best practice change management framework to help you manage any changes effectively;
- specific activities to induce changes in email behaviour;
- examples of what other organizations have done to inculcate some best practice;
- lessons to be learnt from the experiences of other companies.

16.2 Heading for email best practice

The key steps to changing the email culture are summarized in the email best practice change management framework shown in Figure 16.1. Based on the key principles for managing any form of change, they are essentially about deciding:

- what can reasonably be achieved by changing how you use email;
- how can these changes be achieved;
- what results would be expected and how can they be measured;
- who is best placed to manage such a programme.

The steps of the email best practice change management framework are now discussed in more detail.

16.2.1 Action point 1 – Identify the problem and solution

As revealed in Chapter 12, bearing in mind that to some extent the way email is used is a reflection of the corporate culture, this

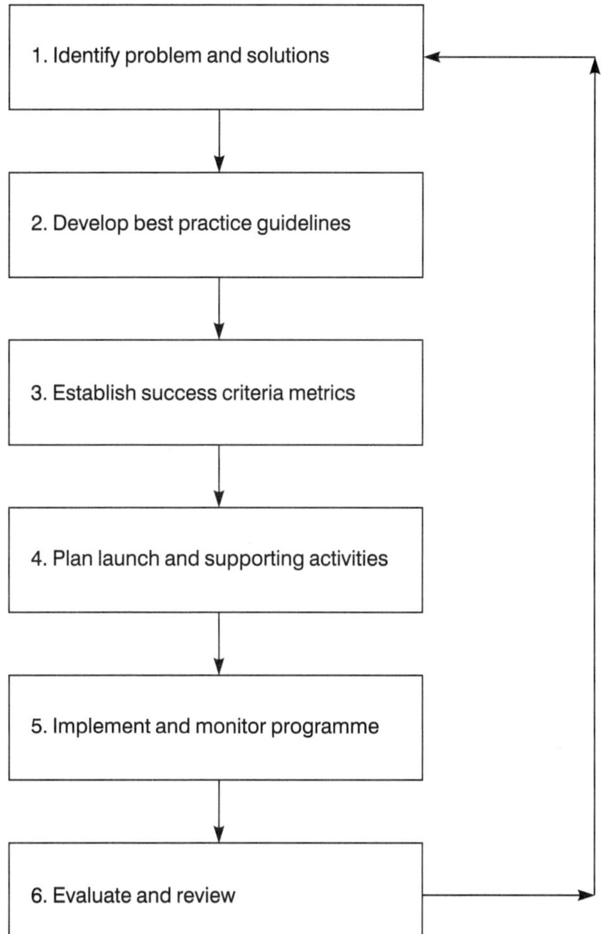

Figure 16.1 Organizational email best practice – change management framework

initially is not as simplistic as it might sound. One of the major problems is that email is often the wallpaper which covers much deeper fissions in the organization. For example, the superficial problem might be the overuse of the 'Reply All' function. Consider a culture that has heavy overtones of 'cover my backside'. You will need either to take some steps to deal with that aspect of the culture or accept that while you can reduce some of the volume of cc'd email there will always be an undercurrent of cc'd mail which is a vestige of the underlying corporate culture.

The ten most common things that wreak havoc on the use of email for corporate communications are shown in Table 16.1.

There are two key ways to identify the common problems people are experiencing with email in your organization. These

Table 16.1 Top ten causes of email rage

1. Overuse of 'Reply All'
2 Too many 'All Employees' emails
3. Overuse of 'cc'd' email
4. Poor grammar and layout
5. Too much reliance on email when another medium would be better, e.g. phone
6. No clear indication of purpose of email
7. Inadequate housekeeping – users taking up valuable storage space on main server
8. Fancy signatures and backgrounds which obscure real purpose of email and take longer to download
9. Attachments – too many and too big
10. Mismatch between the sender's and recipient's priorities and timescales

methods will also help highlight which problems are causing stress and lowering productivity:

- Conventional survey techniques, e.g. focus groups, interviews and questionnaires either to all or a representative sample of employees.
- An inbox audit similar to that described in Chapter 6, but modified to pick up organizational patterns.

> What are the most common sources of email rage in your organization?

Of course this assumes you want only to maintain the status quo as far as management processes are concerned. You could of course, step back and say **email creates an opportunity.** For example, to work differently (maybe more flexibly), to interface with our customers more effectively, to strengthen our brand image, to share more information, to improve our decision making, etc. So how can we capitalize on that opportunity?

The key is to decide what you want to achieve as an organization through the effective use of email, be it either reacting to a known problem or being proactive and creating new opportunities. This is the foundation for your email best practice policy and will enable you to plan an appropriate change management programme.

16.2.2 Action point 2 – Develop email best practice guidelines

Three key aspects you need to consider when developing your email best practice policy are:

- Content
- Ownership
- Format

Content

Only when you have agreed what your organization's goals are, are you really in a position to develop the email behaviour and management policy (or as we call it the email citizen's charter). Chapter 17 contains the 'Nine Ps of Email Best Practice' charter. This is based on the top ten most common sins of the email user. It has been adopted by many organizations either as it stands or adapted to meet their needs as identified from Step 1.

Ownership

Intimately linked to content is ownership of the policy that is both functional ownership (i.e. by which department) and gaining user ownership. This is an important but often overlooked ingredient to success. There are three functions that generally have an interest in email best practice.

Function	Interest
IT/IS	Reducing demands on helpdesk and freeing up server space
Corporate communications (marketing)	Brand image and managing internal communications
Human resources	Training issues and personnel related matters (e.g. protecting privacy)

Wherever possible try to involve a member from each department and one or two employees (preferably one of the worst offenders and one who personifies best practice). Gaining overall buy-in is dealt with in more detail later.

Format

You need to consider what format you will use for publishing the charter. For example, paper, a mouse mat, posters, a booklet, handout, pages on the intranet, etc.? Most organizations use a multiple set of media and generally a combination of mouse mats, paper-based booklets and their intranet (or equivalent, e.g. a Notes Bulletin Board).

The most engaging and ingenious email charter package seen to date by the authors is designed as a football referee's pack complete with whistle, yellow and red card and set of guidance notes (see the Diageo case history on p. 216).

16.2.3 Action point 3 – Establish success criteria metrics

One of the critical factors for engaging people in any form of change management is to establish the goals and milestones, which will tell everyone how well they are performing and how successful the activity has been. Yet again, this cornerstone of effective training and development practice is often cast to the wind when it comes to email best practice. In part this may reflect the difficulty of obtaining hard data such as volumes of email traffic, how many times the 'Reply All' button was used or how many times an email is received with no subject matter.

Some metrics that have been used include monitoring email behaviours before and after an email best practice event:

- volumes of email traffic;
- time spent dealing with email;
- instances of poor practice;
- numbers of a certain type of email which relate to goals, e.g. cc'd;
- levels of email IT fitness;
- attitudes and perceptions about email.

Ways of obtaining some of this data against which the organization as a whole and individual users can benchmark themselves are:

- specialist software such as 'MetaSight' (see Chapter 15);
- inbox audits;
- formal and informal surveys;
- interviews.

The data is generally there for the asking, as we found in Chapters 6 and 13. Some are more inclined to talk about it than others!

16.2.4 Action point 4 – Plan the launch and supporting activities

To create a real enduring change, as indicated, you will need not just an initial launch plan but also a programme of ongoing related activities. None needs to be onerous or resource intense. Typical activities that have achieved successful outcomes are:

Activity	Purpose and usefulness
Email-free time	Making users conscious of using other media, e.g. the phone and thinking about the real need for the proposed email
Inbox housekeeping time	Cleaning up inboxes and freeing up server and disc space
Email rationing	Same as email-free days
Email best practice seminars and workshops	Promoting the new policy/charter and developing users' skills
Email IT fitness drop-in clinics	Boosting users' email IT fitness (often run as one-to-one coaching sessions)
Articles in in-house newsletters and intranets	Re-enforce the message and promote success stories

Who will be your messenger?

Last but by no means least, you must decide how to communicate your message – top-down through some sort of cascade communications programme, simultaneously to every employee, phased across different locations/business units, and so on. The most successful campaigns are led from the top.

16.2.5 Action point 5 – Implement and monitor the programme

The key is to pick activities that will help you achieve your and your organization's (or divisional culture's) goals. This is highlighted in the following case histories and comments. Activities like email-free days are excellent for encouraging users to use more face-to-face communications and to get them to think about the value of sending an email as these quotes illustrate:

> *Email feeds off itself and has generated far more traffic than paper. We have far too much email. We needed a way to signal a change in culture to more face-to-face interventions to resolve issues. We have casual Fridays to re-enforce the concept of a more open free to talk culture. So email free Fridays fitted with this. I have seen a ten to fifteen per cent reduction in the volume of email as a whole and people talking more. We do still use email on a Friday but everyone is just much more conscious and only sends what is really important. I am convinced that if people only sent the really important stuff the email would be self-regulating.*
>
> Andrew Harrison, marketing director, Nestlé Rowntree

> *We wanted to change the way people work together and get them to talk more and move about the business from floor to floor. Some frustrated people took it literally [the email free day] and we needed to educate them that it [the email free day] was about thinking twice before you send an email. If possible don't do it. Otherwise do it. But if you received an email you felt was inappropriate you fined the sender 20p. The money all went to the Comic Relief Charity fund. It worked and still makes people think that you don't need everything in black and white. We encourage trust, and since the new licence agreement there has been more of that and far less 'cover my backside' driven activity. Two years on, we have had a massive change of staff and so we are thinking about doing it again.*
>
> Hilary Smith, PA to chief executive, Camelot

The Camelot experience also highlights the need to build in rewards for best behaviour (or in their case bad behaviour).

At Liverpool Council the volume of email had doubled during the six months January to July 2002. Chief Executive David Henshaw was fed up with the way people used email to pass the buck. David wanted people to 'take control, get agreement and promise of action'. This he felt was often better done over the phone where the importance of the issue could also be conveyed more effectively. Liverpool implemented 'email free Wednesdays'. Affectionately know as a 'Henshawism', the email free Wednesday is managed with a light touch rather than policed. It has been running for three months and has had a very positive reception. 'It gives me a chance to plan my day and clear other work which has built up', says Paul Johnson, Head of the Press Office.

Other organizations have tried a multi-pronged approach with several activities at once.

Case history – Government agency – making email work for you week

This organization chose to have an intense week of email best practice. This was tied into their work–life balance initiatives. They already had some best practice guidelines but these were not being very well used, and email was cited as one of the factors tipping the work–life balance towards the work end. A series of focus groups were held to establish what the problems were and what would help. Based on this, a small team was established to plan some events that would appeal to users right across the organization, at all locations, levels of management and different levels of experience with email. This was what they arranged. It was backed by a poster campaign and a daily message on the organization's intranet designed to promote the theme for the day.

Day	Activity and message
Monday	Seminar – 'Making email work for you'
Tuesday	Email-free day – 'email is not the only way to communicate'
Wednesday	Email drop-in surgeries – boost your email IT fitness
Thursday	Email standards day – send back any emails that don't meet the standards
	High impact email training sessions – writing effective messages
Friday	Good housekeeping day – clear up your inbox and desktop

Yes, there were some negative comments about the email-free day, like 'couldn't operate without email' and 'had to work late the previous night to get all my emails out'. However, overall the week was very successful with comments like these:

> *I found the drop-in centres very helpful, they gave me useful tips on remote working.*
>
> *The 'No email' day was great. It forced me to communicate with people face to face, plus I also gained plenty of exercise commuting between buildings!*

16.2.6 Action point 6 – Evaluate and review

This is always the hard part of any project large or small – the days of reckoning. How did we do? What should we do differently next time? What unfinished business is there? How can we continue the momentum?

Email is still a relatively immature management tool. Add to that staff turnover and it is easy to see how needs will change quite rapidly. Only by constant re-evaluation can you hope to ensure the changes you want meet the business needs.

The evaluation process too is likely to highlight new opportunities to modify processes and potential ways to use new forms of technology (such as personal portals) and to increase further still the effectiveness of email.

16.3 Lessons from other organizations

These two case histories highlight some other ways in which two organizations have implemented best practice.

16.3.1 Case history – Diageo plc

Diageo has positioned itself as 'the leading premium drinks business celebrating life, everyday, everywhere'. In 2002, they launched a company-wide 'new ways of working' programme to change behaviours to match their image as a premium drinks supplier. Three main projects underpinned this initiative: new IT systems to provide better telecommunications and support home working; a more 'funky' environment which is more open and creative (two buildings were merged into one with hotdesking); and a focus on enabling employees to think about what they could get out of the new ways of working.

Effective use of email is crucial but was perceived as poorly used – including too much cc'd mail, inappropriate use, too few had clear titles and too many 'to all employees'.

Their Corporate Communications Division decided to 'hide' the 'all employees' mailing list and launch an email best practice campaign.

This took the form of a football referee's pack complete with whistle and red and yellow warning cards for email misbehaviour. Issued to coincide with the World Cup, they adopted the cascade approach using their 'Function Head' as leader to set the role model, and then desk dropped a pack to every member of staff.

You were free to blow the whistle and issue a warning to anyone whom you felt had used email inappropriately 'to help improve how we [Diageo] use email'.

The best practice handbook *e-mail A Tactical Guide* which comes with the pack has nine principles each with tips on how to achieve them and an appropriate sketch football pitch tactic to deal with being offside.

A prize (a case of drink) was awarded to the person who received the worst 'foul by email' – this was an email which had 14 old documents attached to it.

Charlotte Willcox, director of communications, said:

> *Message titling is now much more exact, and the number of 'reply to all' emails is down. I am saving about an hour a day dealing with my emails. I personally have become much more ruthless. I bin things without opening them. People now know if they want an urgent reply they should ring or see me. Don't rely on email.*
>
> *Reaction has all been positive and having worked with London first now we are going to push it out globally. We hardly ever use 'to all employees' except for the annual results. Any other 'all employees' have to be cleared through my department.*

Charlotte involved the HR and IS departments and the director in charge of the 'new ways of working' project led the exercise.

16.3.2 Case history – Intel

In 1995 Intel launched its 'Your Time' programme to manage email overload. Their IT department had found that some employees were receiving up to 300 emails a day. While people had learnt how to use the technology to send emails few knew how to use it to manage them! They also recognized that the overload was caused not just by individuals but also by the way teams operated. As such there was a complex set of behavioural problems to be resolved and just telling users to curb their email sending was not sufficient. They would have to delve beyond simple exhortations and into actual group behaviour in order to identify causes and define process changes that would eliminate them.

They too worked from the top down and implemented a three part training and development programme:

Awareness training: to propagate a set of predefined organization-wide management expectations.

Group discussions: geared towards identifying bad email habits and their solutions (e.g. they put weekly updates on websites instead of using email).

Skills training: using either a human trainer or a web-based training tool 'to enhance users' proficiency using email clients'.

Covering both the management and technical competence, 'Your Time' took about a year to develop. It was initially rolled out to the Israel site. It has since been deployed worldwide to over 80 000 employees. IT directors were responsible for managing the rollout in partnership with local business managers in order to gain buy-in and to tailor it to local needs.

They tried to stick to the hierarchical 'waterfall' approach although this was not always practical as different business groups had different priorities. In order to keep the programme moving they opted for a less formal approach and allowed groups to use it as appropriate:

> *It has made a difference to the way we use email, the level of abuse and the total volume have decreased. It makes a difference to individuals, so they try to coax others to adopt the principles.*
>
> Adam Sweetman, email product services owner, Intel

'Your Time' is now part of Intel's induction programme.

16.4 Keys to success

Based on these and the earlier case studies, and our own experience, the following eight tips are offered as the keys to successfully creating email best practice across the organization (or a business group):

1 Be very, very clear about the goals and desired outcomes, that is new behaviours and codes of practice, you want to achieve.
2 Decide how you will evaluate the success of your campaign.
3 Pick activities to match your goals.
4 Make it fun.
5 Have the campaign led from the top.
6 Try to tie the campaign to an existing corporate initiative.
7 Reward good play and penalize foul play in a way which is in keeping with the corporate culture.
8 Promote the campaign widely using as many internal communications channels as possible.

16.5 Summary

There are plenty of activities and ways to foster a change in how people use email. Like change initiatives, no matter what the extent of the desired change, it is vital to clearly explain what the benefits of the change to individual users will be. You will also need to set out why the change is necessary, how it will be achieved, what the milestones are *en route* to achieving it and what help is available. Change doesn't happen overnight. One email-free day will not create lasting change. A properly orchestrated series of training and development activities as outlined in this chapter will help successfully ingrain new behaviours into the organization culture.

17 The email citizen's charter for best practice

This book has been about how to harness the power of email to enable you to work smarter both as individuals and organizations no matter how large or small. The previous chapters have provided ways to use email to help you use the two most precious resources you have, your time and your knowledge. In this penultimate chapter we want to share with you the 'Nine Ps of Email Best Practice' that we have developed which encapsulates the essence of this book. We have used it with many people who we have worked with to help them save time, take control of their inbox and in many cases work more productively. The latter may take the form of doing more of the same but more efficiently or in some instances doing things differently and creating new ways of working.

17.1 The Nine Ps of Email Best Practice

Put aside time to deal with emails
Place emails in folders
Pick the right medium
Pen your emails in plain English
Point out the purpose of your emails
Provide time for the recipient
Protect yourself against viruses
Post back unwanted emails
Patrol your use of attachments

17.2 How well does it work?

It inspired me and I had told all my colleagues about some of the ideas . . . I'm using the phone more and talking to people to get things done without a mound of notes. I want to get to the point where when I send something people know it must be important and worth reading.

Human resources director, service organization

I am saving time on my email by also making my responses shorter and not taking on the role of middle man. I send emails back or forward if I know the correct person rather than taking on the problem until I can find the right person.

Vice president, international finance organization

Since the coaching finished, we have all been more restrained in our use of the 'reply to all' button and we have now stopped reaching automatically for the 'send and receive' command.

Programme director, government agency

18 The inbox of the future

The thing with high-tech is that you always end up using scissors.
David Hockney (British Artist), in *The Observer*, 10 July 1994

What does the future hold? With the volume of emails predicted to treble over the next three years, how can we expect to process all the information that is circulating through email? If email continues to be the dominant communications channel, will we have forgotten what it is like to talk to each other by the year 2005? Two of the great promises heralded by email were the paperless office and that business would be conducted much more quickly. The first is clearly a myth when you consider how many of us still print out our emails. And what of those huge multiple attachments? If we keep going as we are, there will hardly be any trees left because they will have all been used to print out our emails.

The second was the ability to do business more quickly (Gates 1999). Gates famously said in his book that the business leaders who succeed will be those 'who take advantage of a new way of doing business based on the increasing velocity of information'. However, some postulate that, in fact, email is the single biggest business disabler and a drain on workers' productivity. They say it has a more debilitating and dangerous effect than alcohol.

Are there signs that in fact as we all become better email citizens and the technology to manage email improves, the size of our inbox will shrink and we will find email starting to fulfil its promises?

To take a look into the future we spoke to Dave Snowden, director of the newly formed IBM Cynefin Centre, which focuses on using human networks to 'enable the emergence of new meaning in organizational complexity'.

18.1 Will there still be email, as we know it now?

The desire for uniformity is ok for accountants but not for communicating. You will need to provide multiple tools to meet different people's needs. What I might find useful you may not. For example, at IBM I use our 'Sametime' real-time messaging system to deal with low-level communications tasks such as agreeing diary arrangements. I might have seven or eight Sametime conversations going on at once. It's like an on-line telephone. It is great for resolving things that can be resolved in real-time. But for a higher level of abstraction I would go to the 'Team Room' and see who has posted information and what discussions are going on. The Team Room is still a piece of work in progress. It is designed to provide team members with a virtual team room in the form of an electronic room through which they can collaborate and store work (e.g. documents). This is the type of work that would normally be sent from one to many users as an email attachment.

We have to move away from having to manage multiple one-to-one conversations through email. To me 30 conventional one-to-one emails are as many as any one person can handle in a day. More than that and we tend to deal with them at a trivial level and answer them quickly just to get rid of them.

Have you ever tried to follow a discussion thread where many people are involved? For me, I usually end up laying all the emails out on the floor and highlighting them by hand with a text marker. Our communications systems-like Team Room enables all the threads of the discussion to be drawn together in one place and one email. This can then be downloaded and read as one document without needing to be on-line all the time. This form of many-to-many communications will be part of the way ahead.

18.2 How are IBM planning to help people be more effective email users?

We've studied how rehabilitation clinics wean people from dependency because email as a one-to-one communications channel has become addictive. Like playing computer games it is destroying the human capacity to interact. We have started to experiment with clients where we take a group of people off email for a month, a sort of 'cold turkey'. They will have to communicate by other means, like the phone and face-to-face meetings (they can use video conferenc-

ing). Then we will bring them back on collaborative systems like our Team Room and habituate them-to-many to many before we bring back email but with no copies or file attachments. That will be done through the tools such as Team Room.

18.3 What about the actual technology to access and process email in whatever form?

Voice recognition and subvocal voice recognition will become increasing important. Subvocal voice recognition being the ability to speak to your PC so no one else can hear, for example when you are in a public place. The smallest PCs are now as small as a PDA and you will soon have true mobility.

Another exciting development will be the ability to access powerful computers from anywhere on demand. For example, you will be able to stand in an airport and rent time on a large machine to process whatever you need to do.

18.4 In the context of electronic communications what business skills do you see as being important for the future?

Our minds work in patterns, but email encourages us to jump around and the result is we deal with things at a trivial level. Eventually the technology of email will merge into the background and there is no doubt that human contact will come back into vogue. In schools I would ban calculators and bring back slide rules: with a slide rule you know if the answer looks right, with calculators you can be wrong and not realize it. Children need to develop a pattern sense for 'rightness' and 'wrongness' at an early age. The key will be the ability to recognize patterns and to be able to identify right and 'wrongness' as we start to use far more narrative type tools to capture knowledge. These are tools which let you capture knowledge in the form of anecdotes which can be indexed and stored and for others to reuse and add more material.

In email you don't have conversations you have information flows. With the evolution of more many-to-many electronic communications media, the art of conversation will again become important.

18.5 Summary

Electronic communications are here to stay. We are on the cusp of the wave; this is the beginning of a new era. Whether the term email will eventually become a synonym for all forms of electronic communications is another matter. What we can be sure of is that we will have learn to work with a range of electronic communications from text messages to virtual team rooms. The skills gained from learning to manage in the email office will stand you in good stead for the future and in many cases put you ahead of the game.

Effective communication now, and increasingly in the future, means balancing indirect electronic communications with the direct or person-to-person communications. Successful communicators will adopt appropriate usage of electronic communications such as email, instant messaging, texts, voicemail and so on. They will balance their use with maintaining and developing good personal relationships with colleagues, competitors and opinion formers. This will be through using direct communications such as regular face-to-face and telephone time with key contacts and by making time for networking and productive meetings. At the end of the day, like many things in life, it's all about achieving balance.

Bibliography

Davis, S. and Meyer, C. (1998). *Blur*. Capstone.

Flynn, N. L. (2000). *The E-Policy Handbook: Designing and Implementing Effective E-mail, Internet and Software Policies*. AMACOM.

Gales, B. (1999). *Business @ The Speed of Light*. Penguin Books.

Grove, A. (1996). *Only the Paranoid Survive*. Currency Doubleday.

Handy, C. (1976). *Understanding Organisations*. Penguin Books.

Hargreaves, G. (1998). *Stress Management*. Marshall Editions.

Hotmail, M. (2001). *Britain, a Nation of E-Literates*. MSN Hotmail.

Kellaway, L. (2002). 'Joys of the lone sewage operative', *Financial Times*, 22 July.

Mallon, R. and Oppenheim, C. (2002). *Aslib Proceedings*, 54(1), 8–22.

Maran, R. (2001). *Teach Yourself Visually Office XP*. Hungry Minds.

Mintzberg, H. (1994). *The Rise and Fall of Strategic Planning*. Prentice-Hall.

Moss Kanter, R. (1992). *Harvard Business Review*, 70(2), 7–8.

Panteli, N. (2002). *Information & Management*, 40, 75–86.

Porter, M. E. and Millar, V. E. (1985). How information gives you competitive advantage. *Harvard Business Review*, July.

Russell, N. and Drew, N. (2001). *ICT Access and Use*. Department for Education and Skills Research Brief No. 252.

Russell, N. and Stafford, N. (2002). *Trends in ICT Access and Use*. Department for Education and Skills Brief No. 358.

Schein, E. (1992). *Organisational Culture and Leadership*. 2nd Edn. Jossey-Bass.

Seeley, M. E. (2000). *Using the PC to Boost Executive Performance*. Gower.

Smith. S. (1975). *The Collected Poems of Stevie Smith*. Penguin Books.

Vinkenburg, C. J., Jansen, P. G. W. and Koopman, P. L. (2000). *Feminine Leadership – A Review of Gender Differences in Managerial Behaviour and Effectiveness*. In: Davidson, M. J. and Burke, R. J. E. (eds) *Women in Management: Current Research Issues Vol. 11*. Sage.

Wang, W. (2001). *Office XP for Dummies*. IDG Books.

Welch, J. (2001). *Jack*. Headline.

Index